MY QUEST FOR

NEFERTITI

Luban, Marianne
My Quest For Nefertiti
ISBN: 978-0-9729524-8-4

Printed in the United States

Pacific Moon Publications
PO Box 275
Ogden, Utah 84402

Illegitimi non carborundum
Ad astra per aspera

INTRODUCTION

I had an interest in the royal mummies of ancient Egypt even as a child. The first real mummified person I ever saw frightened me, however. This was the well-preserved remains of an anonymous male at the old Science Museum of St. Paul, Minnesota, the city where I grew up. The building in which the exhibits were housed was a rather gloomy-appearing old mansion, inside and out. I went there on a field trip with my grade school and the ancient priest was the first dead person I had seen up close. The sight of him made death a reality and I confess to having a sleepless night on account of a new realization. Death was not pretty and it was final. It lasted not only for 3,000 years, the given age of that mummy, but for eternity. Death was the constant stalker of us all and we could escape his clutches for only so long. Some were lucky enough to have a long life and others were not so fortunate. Regardless, we would all disappear forever at some point, none of us receiving awed visitors every day like the nameless Egyptian. I would have to become accustomed to the idea of my own mortality.

The old Science Museum of St. Paul building [formerly the Merriam mansion]

Yet, after this initial shock, I could add mummies to my list of things about the ancient civilization that fascinated me. Just previously, on another school outing, I had been introduced to the Egypt of antiquity by the film, "The Ten Commandments", the one starring Charlton Heston, released in 1956. It was a revelation of a place and time that must have touched something deep within me. Sitting in that movie theater, I felt that I was viewing something to which I had a connection. The movie had to do with me, who I was, and who I always would be. Now I knew it, although I had no inkling when I walked through the door of the theater. But why Egypt? I couldn't understand it, but I know the other Heston picture, "Ben-Hur", [1959] didn't affect me like that, although I found it quite wonderful. In fact, even as a kid I knew it was a far better movie than "The Ten Commandments"—but it didn't strike that same chord.

I didn't start reading every book I could find about the Rome of the Caesars, but I began to devour those written about ancient Egypt in the libraries to which I had access. In the beginning, I feel sure that the ones with the most photos were the attraction. A few years later I brought home books about all the early civilizations but the Egyptian was unquestionably my favorite. It was the one in which I eventually attained a real level of expertise.

My recollection of novels set in the period is scant and I doubt very much that as many existed in my youth as do now. However, there were two that I considered fabulous. They were "Mara Daughter of the Nile" and "Pharaoh", both written by Eloise Jarvis McGraw. They were set in the reign of Thutmose III. I couldn't comprehend why no one had made a movie about them, but I did like the one based on Mika Waltari's novel, "The Egyptian" [1954]. Here was a film that took place during the reign of Akhenaten, the heretic pharaoh, although he and his queen, Nefertiti, did not get much screen time.

I can't say I was particularly focused on Nefertiti

then, although I, like everyone else on the planet, was impressed by her famous bust, arguably the most recognized piece of statuary in the world. Nefertiti is uniquely and breathtakingly beautiful. Even Adolf Hitler was in awe of her loveliness. The bust, which found its way from Egypt to Berlin, is said to have been fashioned by a sculptor and artist named Thutmose, whose gift can be likened to that of Michelangelo. Thanks to Egyptological research, we have more information about him today than we previously did.

The trouble with Nefertiti, as far as I was concerned, was that so little was known about her. Was she Egyptian? Was she foreign, possibly from the land of Mitanni to the east? Why did she wear a flat-topped blue crown never before seen on the head of a queen of Egypt and never after? Where did this headdress originate or what influenced its creation? No one could answer these questions with assurance in the days of my youth. All that was certain was that she was the chief wife of Akhenaten, gave birth to six daughters—and then disappeared from the record. But there were some tantalizing things that scholars couldn't quite comprehend. Nefertiti was sometimes depicted in a way that suggested she had power beyond that of a mere consort. On the other hand, there were also some clues indicating Nefertiti had fallen out of favor with her husband, her place having been assumed by her eldest daughter. Or perhaps she was edged out by a young male, whom the king elevated to a coregent, Akhenaten now exhibiting his latent homosexuality!

About the time I was in junior high school, I wrote

a letter to Professor Keith C. Seele of Chicago's Oriental Institute [I had read and re-read his work, "When Egypt Ruled the East", co-authored with Georg Steindorff, and first published in 1942], asking him what it took to become an Egyptologist. Seele actually replied, bless his memory, and explained the process. I found it rather daunting. So many years were involved! I was a young person who loved to read. Our house had a screened-in front porch and, in summer, I could spend hours sitting in there with a book in my hands every day. I believed I knew myself and that my inclinations were already set. I

Our house on York Avenue on the east side of St. Paul. It is no longer there. All the houses on the block have vanished. Only my school, Johnson High, [roof projecting above the house next to ours] remains.

had already discovered the opera via recordings that one

could bring home from the library I haunted—and that became a life-long passion. But one thing I didn't like—or so I thought—was studying and being stuck in school.

Many years later, after watching the movie, "Peggy Sue Got Married", I, like many others, wished I could go back to my high school age, as happened to Peggy Sue, if only for a day. But, at the time, I didn't like going to school. I didn't exactly hate it, but the whole thing bored me. I don't really know why. I got good grades, for the most part, had friends, and other kids didn't give me much grief. I think one of the reasons that high school didn't have much appeal for me is because I was not attracted to boys my own age. Because of my in-

It began here. The Arlington Hills Branch of the St. Paul Public Library System, the place where I obtained most of my reading and listening materials as a child and teen. I loved going there. It ceased operation as a library in 2014. Photo by McGhiever of Minnesota.

terests, I felt I was too old for them and looked it, too. When I was sixteen, I could have passed for twenty and older men wanted to date me.

I wouldn't have minded going out with some of them, but my parents wouldn't allow it, so I didn't have much of a social life. Of course, I don't blame them. My European mom and dad also believed that everybody over the age of sixteen should have at least a part time job, so I didn't have any time to spare for extra-curricular activities at school, either. Once I reached the age where I could legally work, I was expected to buy all my own clothes, cosmetics, records—whatever I needed or wanted. Since I lived in their house, I was ruled by the whims of my parents [at which I soon rebelled] and, as a result, high school was not that much fun for me. Most evenings I didn't get home from work until around 9 pm, having taken the bus to my job right after my last class. Then I still had to do homework. Fortunately, I was very strong in those days but I often felt the lack of sleep.

Naively, I projected that college would be just as dull and so the long years of higher education described by Professor Seele, if one wanted a career in Egyptology, began to have less and less appeal. Since I was an attractive young lady, my parents simply figured I'd soon get married [in that era many girls went from high school graduation straight to the altar] and nobody encouraged me to go to college except my school counselor. He even came to the house in an attempt to sell the idea to my mother and father—and to me. My test scores were very high and I could probably get a scholarship.

But my parents were unconvinced that academia

and I were a good match. Perhaps I struck them as too flamboyant and flashy with my makeup and fancy bouffant hairstyles. Not that I appeared too outrageous. I didn't have any piercings except in my ear lobes and I didn't dye my hair weird colors—at least not on purpose. My mode of dress was typical for the 1960's and that was conservative. Yet, in my senior year, I was voted by the class as one of two "Biggest Nonconformists".

I was delighted, but when I showed the school paper to my mother, she was less than pleased. "It's not good to be too different" she warned, but I rather thought that not being afraid to be myself and have my own opinions was the best thing in the world. By then I knew that I could never win the approval of my parents because the real problem was I was simply much too different from *them*. I think my folks knew I was intelligent but I suspected why their ambitions for me were so low. I could never do them proud in a way that they or their circle of friends would find impressive.

Was there anything less down-to-earth than wanting to become an Egyptologist? Hadn't I once expressed a longing to follow that path? My parents simply couldn't comprehend such notions. Once, my mom even told me to stop telling people that was what I wanted to do when I grew up. Well, they asked! Now, as a teenager, I didn't seem to know what I wanted. Since I spent a lot of time scribbling and, after that, at my little typewriter, it was starting to look like my imagination was running away with me. Years into the future, I read a letter my mom had written to her own mother back in Europe. Grandma had saved all the letters. In it was the statement, "*Marianne is the phlegmatic one. [!] Real time does not count for her. Truthfully, I don't know what you could send Marianne. Maybe a few notebooks. She is always writing stories and is always running out of paper.*"

Phlegmatic was hardly the term to describe me then or now. I was a born romantic—and why my mother failed to characterize me as such is baffling. How many dispassionate teens write fiction and listen to grand opera? I certainly thought I lived in the real world, as the long hours I put in at school and at work seemed a necessary but time-consuming intrusion on matters that occupied my thoughts and imagination. On the other hand, I found the city in which I lived very interesting at that time. On weekends, my friends and I walked or biked for miles just to explore it.

But Mom had a point. I always had one foot in another time—the distant past. Often it seemed more real to me than the present, more fascinating, anyway. The thirst for knowledge about Egypt was a constant in my existence, one that was never interrupted once it began.

Much later, the dynamics in the household that failed to form me in its image changed, and one of my younger sisters became a doctor of psychology and a college professor. From then on, higher education became a priority in our extended family. No one was criticized for not wanting to travel that road, but everyone who did was encouraged and supported.

As for me, I had a good voice and thought perhaps I should do something with that. Learning how to sing better, making music, seemed like more fun than continuing my formal education. But I managed to sidetrack myself from doing even that for quite some time and allowed the prophesy of my parents to come true. Like Peggy Sue, I got married young. By the time I was twenty-one I had two little daughters. Meanwhile, though, I continued to read about Egypt, kept up with the new books—and studied all the cultures of the ancient Near East. The University of Minnesota offered adult education courses and there I pursued writing and art history.

When I had reached the age of twenty-five, I did go to college, several of them, but as a private student of the professors of voice associated with those institutions. By then I was a youthful single parent and soon discovered that vocal music, the operatic kind, requires tremendous dedication and hard work, almost to the exclusion of everything else. A woman with young children doesn't have the time to put in the hours of practice [including the piano in order to learn the required level of musicianship], especially if she has to work outside the home. So I had to settle for becoming a semi-professional soprano on a very modest scale, even though my teachers told me the voice and talent were certainly not lacking. I sometimes got paid as a soloist but my singing career never really materialized.

In brief, I became a Jane of all trades. I had a knack for writing and my short stories had been accepted by magazines. In fact, they had all been accepted, so I felt sufficiently encouraged to write a short fiction collection. Since I had been paid for my work, it seemed to me I could consider myself a professional author. By this time it was the 1980's. I had married again, and had two more daughters. These were still very small girls when I turned my dining room table into a desk, set up my newer typewriter, and wrote every chance I got until the collection was finished. Sometimes I had to stop in mid-sentence in order to attend to something else. The process took quite awhile but, in 1990, the work was published by the Minneapolis-based Coffee House Press under the title, "The Samaritan Treasure". It was nominated for a prize by the Minnesota Book Awards committee in the category of fiction [but didn't win] and described in an anthology called "500 Great Books By Women".[1]

During this same period my personal life got increasingly complicated and I didn't do much writing for a long time, not taking on another book project until about the year 2000, after I had moved to Los Angeles. But I had learned discipline and dedication and knew that I could accomplish something if I applied myself to it. Even during the chaos of the 1990's, I studied the Egyptian language without ceasing. I realized that, if one wanted to understand the ancient Egyptians, one had to know their language, too. It is probably the most difficult challenge I have ever met, but I got hooked on Egyptian and couldn't give it up, didn't want to. Of course, the study of it doesn't end because the subject is too vast. Egyptian isn't Spanish. The graphic system has hundreds of signs which have to be memorized and the grammar is complex. I started with Middle Egyptian but there is Neo-Egyptian, Demotic, and Coptic, as well.

---

1   Bauermeister and Larsen, Penguin Books [1994].

Most significantly, I learned that I love to study, do research, and like to learn something new each day. I didn't know myself very well at all as a high school girl. In retrospect, I realize that all the reading I did even then was a kind of scholarship, only one lacking any real discipline or objective. University was definitely my milieu and I probably would have liked it much more than I suspected I would. But, over the ensuing years, I have discovered other things, too. One needn't be formally educated to become learned and those with degrees aren't necessarily highly intelligent or imaginative. In a field like Egyptology, the doctors can be just as wrong in their theories as the amateurs— although perhaps for different reasons.

Regardless, what most people who achieve a PhD in Egyptology soon learn is that they'll never become famous or amount to anything special in their chosen profession. They won't become Indiana Jones. In fact, they're fortunate if they can find a job related to their degree. In order to be a great Egyptologist you must have imagination, a logical mind, and you must write well. Or you must be incredibly lucky—like Howard Carter, the discoverer of the tomb of Tutankhamun. Carter, by the way, learned to become an Egyptologist by doing. He had come to Egypt as an artist and not an excavator. Some of the ones with sheepskins become very well-known to Egyptophiles by appearing on television as talking heads or by looking into nooks and crannies with flashlights in documentaries. But that doesn't necessarily mean they are respected by their peers. There are many Egyptologists around the world but only a very few at any given time who are swaying opinion via their papers and books.

A good Egyptologist has the open, inquiring mind of a detective, knows how to make the puzzle pieces fit. One must have the ability to notice things that others have missed or at least interpret them in a novel and convincing fashion. We have been fortunate to have learned from such outstanding scholars of the 20th Century and today.

Should you happen to have the ability to make some novel observations but lack a formal degree, what you will get is a lot of stick —particularly from those you encounter on the Internet who never come up with anything original. Lacking imagination, they're not capable of it. Resentment will attack you from all sides and sometimes your ideas will be appropriated without attribution by various persons who think you don't count as a source. Mostly, academia will simply ignore you because it prefers to be an exclusive club. Only an act of God will move it to acknowledge your contribution. And yet, sometimes, even when the very finger of God has pointed out the way via science, academia will persist in its stubborn refusal to see the light.

That is not to say that the world of Egyptology lacks kind, even nurturing, individuals. I know they exist, as I have been the recipient of their encouragement, advice, as well as difficult-to-find materials.

This book reflects my cerebral search for Queen Nefertiti of the 18th Dynasty, putting my thoughts in online papers and blog posts over the years. Some of them are wholly or partially included in this book. Not only did I seek the mummy of Nefertiti, I also have tried to define her life by logically reviewing the clues. Time has proved to be on my side, I believe. As the evidence slowly mounts, I feel I am being vindicated in my theory rather than otherwise. We shall see what the future brings.

Chapter One

THE TOMB

Beyond my own introduction to Egyptology and why I failed to pursue it as a career, the story of my life is of little relevance except that I have lived long enough to learn some new facts about the twilight years of the 18th Dynasty.

For some decades of my existence, there were few major revelations, although plenty of excavating. The home of Akhenaten and Nefertiti had been an archaeological site long before I was born. Ludwig Borchardt dug at at Tell el Amarna, the ruins of the ancient city of Akhetaten, prior to World War I. John Pendlebury, the Englishman, continued the work close to the time of the Second Great War. This was, one might say, the beginning of the obsession with all things pertaining to Amarna. The findings of these archaeologists and their teams led to arguments by scholars, especially over whether or not there had ever been a coregency between Akhenaten and his father, Amunhotep III.

In between, in 1922, the world went into a media frenzy. The tomb of a little known pharaoh had been uncovered by Howard Carter and his sponsor, Lord Carnarvon. KV62 in the Valley of the Kings was filled with so many amazing treasures, so much gold, that it was rather mind-boggling. No one had imagined that the Egyptian rulers possessed such items as emerged from that tomb because their art never even hinted at their existence. Nobody, for instance, had any idea that there were ancient Egyptian shoemakers with the sophisticated degree of skill displayed by Tutankhamun's sandals or that the royals wore garments covered with sparkling sequins.

Yet, unfortunately, KV62 yielded few texts to add to the knowledge of the life of its owner or his family. Those that existed on certain pieces proved difficult to interpret. It was as though this extended period defied anyone to really understand it. No other era in Egyptian history was so frustrating.

After Carter's find and its publication, debates centered around Tutankhamun, as well. Since he was a successor of Akhenaten, how was he connected to him? Who were the boy's parents? It was known that he was the son of a king because that was written in stone—but which one? Some believed Tutankhamun's sire was Akhenaten and the mother a secondary wife of that pharaoh named Kiya. Others preferred Amunhotep III and his daughter/queen, Sitamun, for the parents.

16

Sitamum was the eldest daughter of the pharaoh and his chief consort, Queen Tiye. She was elevated from princess to junior queen in Year 30 of her father.

Next to nothing was known about Kiya and hardly more about Tutankhamun, himself. He became king at an early age and died while still under twenty. That summed him up in the beginning but Tut, ever since the discovery of his incredible tomb, has continued to surprise. In 1996, there was another breakthrough. French Egyptologist, Alain Zivie, uncovered the tomb of Tutankhamun's nurse, called Maya. At that time I wrote these words online:

"Long ago there was a boy who found himself on the throne during a time of turbulence. He reigned about a decade and did not distinguish himself in any particular fashion. This Tutankhamun is no empire builder, no son of the god Montu to strike fear in the hearts of his enemies. His portraits often show him as soft and effeminate or just wistfully beautiful. He appears tainted by a decadence for which he was not responsible. Tutankhamun died very young without an heir to succeed him. He is neither lauded nor reviled,[2] then shortly forgotten. Soon the memory of Tutankhamun, though a king of Egypt, is not even a faint echo in the vast canyon of time. He seems fated to be cheated of the immortality conferred upon other kingly names. He is no Ozymandias to inspire a poet of any age.

---

2 The monuments of Tutankhamun, possibly even his original tomb, were usurped by his successors, however. His immediate successors did not steal his treasures, on the other hand, and after that the whereabouts of KV62 seems to have been forgotten, probably aided by some flooding in the Valley of the Kings.

17

But this unsung young man manages, instead, to cheat time. In a way, it seems he was just biding his, waiting for a man named Howard Carter to be born. And, truly, it does seem as if Carter was born to do just this one thing—reclaim Tutankhamun from the depths of obscurity. Coming forth once again into daylight with the same blaze of gold with which he descended 3,000 years before, the pharaoh dazzles our century. But it is not just the lavish use of precious metal and the wonderful treasures that fascinate us. It is also something captured by a genius of a goldsmith in a portrait. Thanks to him we have to perceive Tut as being perfectly immediate, human and vulnerable. Gold was thought to be the flesh of the gods and, in the way that great art has of being more real than life, we can only view the withered face of the dead boy as an artifact beside such artistry. On the other hand, we are oddly certain that no artist, however great, could have given us portraits of men such as Seti I and his son, Ramesses, that could have the impact on us that their own dead faces have achieved.

However, various fateful combinations of factors made King Tut, more fortunate in death than in life, the most famous Egyptian ruler ever. Still, his fabulous tomb, while revealing to us the extent of the wealth and beauty surrounding the kings of Egypt, tells us nothing much about Tut, himself. As with all superstars, though, rumors, gossip, and theories arose concerning his origins, life and death. He has even been imbued with the ability to avenge himself upon those who dared to disturb his anonymous slumber. And so King Tut, such as is known about him personally, and the circumstances surrounding

18

his re-discovery, became a kind of industry for three-quarters of a century.

But just when one was sure the young king would keep all his secrets forever, 75 years to the dot later, it looks like he will tantalize us by revealing a bit more about himself to a whole new generation, all those who initially dealt with his resurrection themselves being dead. A French archaeological team has recently uncovered a new tomb at Saqqara, a few kilometers west of Cairo. It belongs to one Maya, the wet nurse of the pharaoh, Tutankhamun. From this tomb, it is hoped that Egyptologists will finally discover who the actual parents of the boy-king were,[3] as this has been hotly debated for seven decades. This is Tut flexing his powers, proving himself, indeed, the Master of Time—or perhaps just timing."

During my youth and middle-age I do not remember anyone strongly advocating in print that Nefertiti may have been the mother of Tutankhamun, although I am certain the possibility was considered among other scenarios. Mostly, I seem to recall the young monarch referred to as the son-in-law of Akhenaten, due to his marriage to Ankhesenpaaten, later Ankhesenamun, the third daughter of the heretic.

Another son-in-law was a certain Smenkhkare, for whom the term "ephemeral" appears to have been coined, it is so often used to describe him and his reign. This man had married Merytaten, the eldest daughter of Akhenaten and Nefertiti. But Julia Samson,[4] for one,

---

3 The tomb of Maya did not reveal the information.
4 Samson, Julia, **Nefertiti and Cleopatra: Queen-Monarchs of**

19

believed there was no actual male named Smenkhkare Djeserkheperu, that he was Nefertiti under a new name. This was mainly due to the fact that, at Amarna, a name that appeared in the cartouches of the queen was "Neferneferuaten".

Yet, in the very same time frame, there was obviously a king called Ankhkheperure Neferneferuaten, as well. Ankhkheperure was also the prenomen of Smenkhkare and so Samson concluded the latter was Nefertiti in male garb à la Hatshepsut. Merytaten had to be her nominal Great Royal Wife. In the earlier part of the dynasty, Hatshepsut had, indeed, been depicted wearing the clothing of a man once she made herself pharaoh, but Hatshepsut certainly did not have her own daughter, Neferure, shown standing beside her as the queen of "Maatkare", her throne name. [5]

Therefore, if Julia Samson was correct, Nefertiti and Merytaten would have been the first same-sex king and consort in all of Egyptian history up to that point. Few were convinced of this and Smenkhkare continued to be largely viewed as a prince of the dynasty—but just whose son he happened to be was also uncertain. Both Amunhotep III and Akhenaten were candidates for his father. But, again, there were those who viewed Ankhkheperure Smenkhkare as the coregent and lover of the bisexual Akhenaten.

At least there was no doubt as to the parents of Akhenaten, who began his reign as the fourth

---

Ancient Egypt [London, 1990]

5   The title of Neferure was "god's wife", a religious one .bestowed on the daughters of kings.

Amunhotep, his given name. His mother was most certainly Queen Tiye. Some of his sisters were known[6] and the name of an elder brother was Thutmose, after his grandfather. Due to the death of this brother at what must have been a young age, Akhenaten was able to become the successor of Amunhotep III.

The marriage of the latter to Tiye was seen as a kind of Cinderella story, prince falls in love with commoner and makes her the first lady of the kingdom in due course. On account of some commemorative scarabs of Amunhotep and the discovery of the tomb of Yuya and Thuya, the parents of Queen Tiye, a few things were known about her family. Yuya was a priest of Min at the town of Akhmim and Thuya also was associated with the cult of this deity. A son of Thuya was the Second Prophet of Amun, called Aanen, who was attested more than once and who had a tomb on the hill Sheikh abd el Qurna. Most likely Yuya, who had become a very great man in Egypt because of his new royal connections, was his father, but there was some doubt. An Egyptian writer, Ahmed Osman, saw Yuya as being identical with the Joseph of the Hebrew Bible, a foreigner who had risen to the highest position in the land, second only to the pharaoh.[7]

Of Nefertiti's background nothing was known. Over time, a consensus was formed that the queen must have been the daughter of Ay, an official who bore the title of "it nTr", meaning "father of the god", which was once viewed as being the term for a father-in-law of a

---

6   Sitamun, Isis, Henuttaneb, Nebetah, and possibly Baketaten.
7   Osman, Ahmed, **Stranger In the Valley of the Kings** [1988]

pharaoh. As it happened, there was a man styled "it nTr", who really was the father-in-law of a king—and that was Yuya. Today it is recognized that "it nTr" could also be a priestly title and that of a mentor to a young ruler or prince.

In the Amarna tomb of Ay and Tey, his wife, there is no mention of Nefertiti being the daughter of Ay. It does say that Tey was a nurse of "the goddess", meaning Nefertiti. That eliminated Tey from being the mother of the queen, so those who wished Ay to be her father had to postulate a previous [dead] wife for him. Also depicted in the same tomb is Mutnodjmet, who is therein called a sister of the queen—but it is not specified how this girl was related to Ay or Tey. In the Egyptian language, the term for "sister" could also mean "female cousin". So nothing absolute could be gleaned from the tomb texts about the parents of Nefertiti but nothing much could be ruled out, either. Since Ay was obviously a very important man in the regime of Akhenaten, it was quite likely that he was related to the royal family somehow. That he was a brother of Queen Tiye was the most popular position. If Ay was the father of Nefertiti, that would have made Akhenaten and Nefertiti first cousins.

The marriages of first cousins were common enough in ancient Egypt, one feels, because they were hardly rare in much more modern Egypt. To the Europeans and Americans studying Egyptian history, such an arrangement seemed preferable to the brother/sister unions of previous kings and queens of the dynastic period. However, people got a bit squeamish when hints were uncovered that Akhenaten might have married his own daughters and actually had children with them in his protracted effort to get a son and heir.

Not only that, but Neferkheperure Akhenaten may even have produced a daughter with his own widowed mother, Queen Tiye! This notion was entertained due to the fact that there was a little girl shown at Akhetaten, usually in the company of the dowager, whose name was Baketaten. The latter was only styled "king's daughter of his body" and never "king's sister" and some scholars wondered why.

Had this child been, instead, depicted as even a half-grown girl, Baketaten would have aroused no suspicion. But there she stood, looking as little as the king's known younger daughters. Did Akhenaten have

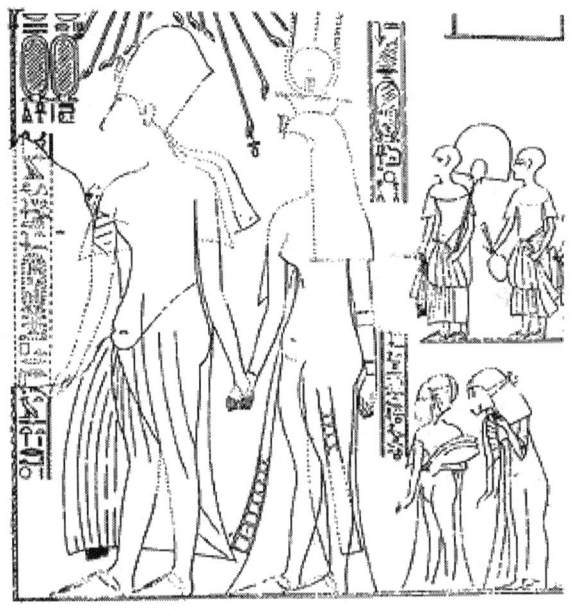

Akhenaten and Queen Tiye, followed by Baketaten

23

no boundaries whatsoever where his sex life was concerned?[8] He already had two certain wives, the beauteous Nefertiti and the mysterious Kiya, perhaps also attractive—and probably nameless concubines, as well, like his father before him. So what was it that the pharaoh was trying to prove? And just how old was this mother of his, anyway?

In addition, there were two other little girls named Merytaten-tasherit and Ankhesenpaaten-tasherit. Their names indicated that they were the smaller versions of the first and third Amarna princesses. Who were their parents? Mostly, Akhenaten was pointed to as having fathered them on those very daughters. How much incest could this family bear and what could the consequences have been for the relationship between Akhenaten and Nefertiti? And what was the effect on the mental and physical health of the children?

It was quite unsettling and both Egyptologists and enthusiasts began to form a picture of Akhenaten that engendered dislike. Queen Nefertiti emerged as a victim of such indulgences on the part of her husband. First, she had been forced to become the consort of an ugly man—she who might have been the loveliest girl in all of Egypt. Then she fell out of favor as soon as her eldest daughter reached puberty, Merytaten replacing her mother as the object of the king's preference. It appeared that Egyptian men liked them young, very young, if a beauty like Nefertiti could be eclipsed when she was

---

8   However, on a lintel in the Amarna tomb of Huya there is a scene depicting a seated Amunhotep III, facing Tiye and Baketaten, which rather indicates they were viewed as a family group.

probably no more than twenty-six.

Finally—or so it was believed—Nefertiti died around Year 14, probably of a broken heart and spirit. All the incestuous license and possibly even homosexuality practiced by Akhenaten had doubtless caused a rift between the royal pair. They were portrayed as holding hands in an important tableau that represented a great occasion taking place in Year 12, but the reign still had five more years to run. Worst of all, Nefertiti had lost her second daughter, Meketaten, soon after Year 12. Akhenaten was blamed for this tragedy, as well, it being concluded that an infant in a mourning scene was borne

by Meketaten, who died as a result. Her immature body had been fatally ruined in order to give her father the son he lacked. If the queen had actually committed suicide after these crushing blows, she could hardly be blamed.

Grafton Elliot Smith, MD, KG, FRCP

This was more or less the situation, the theories, suspicions, and sentiments surrounding Nefertiti and her circumstances—about the time that I began to really wonder about her in earnest.

It had to do with this volume, the source of my inspiration: "The Royal Mummies", published in 1912, became a kind of bible for those of us interested in the mummified remains of the deceased pharaohs and their relatives. It represented the observations of a man named Sir Grafton Elliot Smith, who was a medical doctor and professor of anatomy at the Cairo School of Medicine during the time when imperial Britain still occupied Egypt under a protectorate policy. Smith was born in Australia in 1871 and died in London in 1937.

Dr. Smith's investigation of the royal mummies came about due to the discoveries of two caches of what remained of the great ones of ancient Egypt. The first one was found by natives at Deir el Bahri and its clearing was done under the supervision of Emil Brugsch, a curator attached to the Boulaq Museum in Cairo. This took place in 1881. TT320, as it is now called, contained the mummies of many persons, including great pharaohs like Thutmose III, Seti I, and Ramesses II.

The second cache, secreted in KV35, the tomb of Amunhotep II, was the one that interested me more. Before Victor Loret entered this tomb in 1898, he already knew there were shabtis of Amunhotep II on the market in Egypt and in Europe and had been for years. So had many other pieces from 18th Dynasty nobility burials. Mohammed Abd el Rassoul, head of the famous Gurneh family long suspected of trafficking in antiquities, had even boasted that he knew of the existence of an undiscovered tomb of a king—and KV35 was surely it. In other words, this tomb had already been plundered in modern times before Loret began his investigation.

Originally cut for one 18th Dynasty pharaoh and perhaps his immediate family, KV35, as a royal cache, had more order to it than TT320. The successors of Aakheperure Amunhotep II were there—but not all of them. Then the order of succession skipped directly to the end of the 19th Dynasty, but not beginning with King Merneptah, son of Ramesses II, as it should have done, as his forebears were in TT320. Added to the 19th Dynasty rulers were some later pharaohs of the 20th Dynasty. A few other nameless persons were also included.

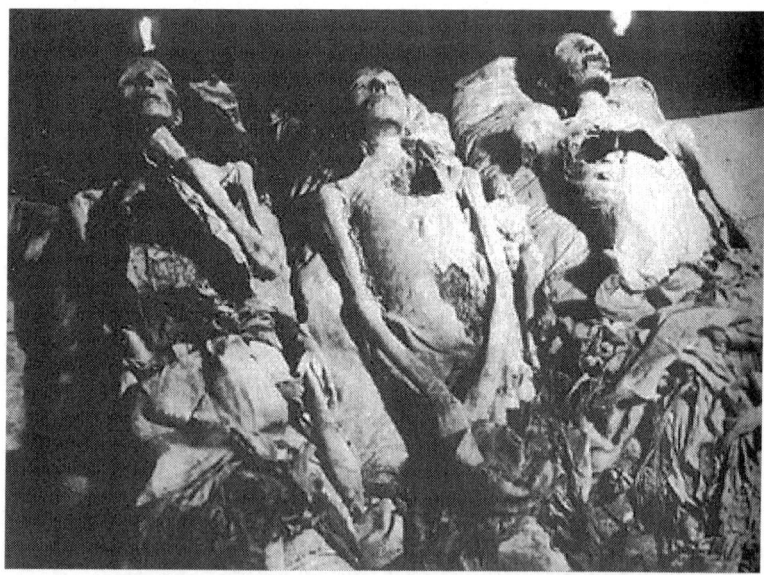

Much speculation has been offered regarding the anonymous corpses, sans coffins, lying in a side chamber,

"The Elder Lady", "The Young Prince", and "The Younger Lady". Loret found these mummies neatly arranged but quite naked with their bandages lying in tatters all around them, whereas the nine mummies in another room appeared, for the most part, to be wrapped up the way the restorers of the 21st Dynasty had left them.[9]

Victor Loret [1859-1946]

It is difficult to believe the three royal persons, lying on the floor, were deposited in KV35 in such a state of disarray by any reburial commission of ancient times. One would have to wonder why no replacement coffins

9   The following account is based on an online article, written by me in 2001 on my defunct website. An inscription on the mummy of Amunhotep III, found in KV35, records a date of restoration of the mummies in Year 12 or 13 of Smendes.

were provided for them like all the other royal mummies. Whether or not something of value was left upon the trio of mummies from antiquity, we shall probably never know. That they were members of the immediate family of Amunhotep II was thought likely for many years after the discovery of the cache. Since the floor of KV35 was thick with debris, something of their burials could have remained—sold to private collectors. As for the kingly mummies in KV35—the Rassouls evidently were never motivated to bother with them. Their coffins appeared very poor and were covered with a heavy pall of dust. Or perhaps the truth was that the clan of tomb-robbers never had time to pay them much attention. Only Amunhotep II remained in his own sarcophagus, and even this monarch had not been disturbed in modern times, but still wore the funerary wreath left by the restoring priests. Later on, however, someone stole the great bow buried with the king—the one he had boasted only he could pull.

Victor Loret, as it turned out, was never able to do a scientific evaluation of KV35. Following three weeks of clearing the tomb and packing the mummies in crates, Loret loaded them onto a boat and brought them to the Museum at Ghiza. This proved a waste of time. According to Howard Carter's memoirs: *"In consequence, an administrative question arose and he received orders to replace them in the tomb."*

Loret's ire and frustration can easily be imagined, yet he had no choice but to comply. KV35 presumably remained re-sealed until Gaston Maspero, another Frenchman who had taken Loret's place as director of the

Service des Antiquities, came to remove some of the mummies in 1901. In this task he had the aid of Carter, who wrote: "*I replaced the mummy of Amenophis II in his sarcophagus, with the flowers and foliage upon him as they were originally discovered; the three naked mummies I put back in the side treasury where they were found; and the mutilated mummy upon the frame of a model boat, in the Antechamber.*[10] *With regard to the other nine mummies, the plan was changed. It was decided to transport them on a special government steamer to the Ghiza Museum near Cairo.*"

After this the tomb of Amunhotep II was opened to the public and in November of 1901 it was entered by tomb-robbers yet again.

Loret claimed that he had intended to do an in-extenso examination of the KV35 mummies, complete with x-rays, in Cairo, but that this opportunity had been denied him under the circumstances. Because the bodies and their containers were lined up in such close proximity in their side-chamber,[11] the Egyptologist wrote that he decided to take down a wall of stones that had partly sealed the doorway and to have the mummies and receptacles carried into the "*grande salle*" of the tomb. Victor Loret indicated that it was not until after the nine mummies had been moved that photographs were taken and "*each mummy measured, described, examined in all their details*". Certain inscriptions were appraised by

---

10 The boat was stolen when KV35 was robbed and the anonymous mummy was smashed to pieces within the tomb.

11 Loret first commented that the chamber was "rather large", being three metres by four.

candle-light on the wrappings. In the words of Loret: *"I copied them patiently, mechanically, without giving myself time to study them in depth."*

The excavator did his best to assure us that he took every precaution under the circumstances. At any rate, no detailed records of his work in the Valley of the Kings were ever published. The most comprehensive account we have of his discovery of KV35 is in the form of an article, "Le Tombeau D'Amenophis II", printed in the Bulletin De L'Institut Egyptien in May of 1898, some months after Loret entered this tomb. There, he tries to convey his excitement upon first realizing the importance of what he had found in the side-chamber:

"Everywhere cartouches! Here, the prenomen of Siptah; there, the names of Seti II; nearby, a long inscription including the complete titulary of Thutmose IV. We had stumbled upon a royal cache comparable to that of Deir-el-Bahri." And... *"After Thutmose IV, Amenophis III. Following the son of Amenhotep II, his grandson. The genealogical series continued, which had so well commenced with Thutmose III[12] and Amenophis II, and which would finish with [Akhenaten]."*

Loret caused the doorway of the side-chamber to be walled-up again *"after having taken notes and made notations."* However, right after that he wrote: *"The nine coffins were quickly packed up and put into crates."* Loret gives assurances of careful documentation but, as was mentioned, never published his notes or best photographs. The photos we have all seen of the three mysterious mummies, lying side by side upon packing

---

12 Loret had previously explored the tomb of Thutmose III.

boxes, candles at their heads, were found years later in a souvenir shop in Cairo. Although Loret's piece in the Bulletin De L'Institut Egyptien is extremely well-written and amply descriptive, I have not been able to view his notebook containing the only on site jottings that Loret actually made concerning the royal corpses. In his paper they read as follows [quoting Loret in my English translation]:

1. Coffin and matching lid. Written is the name of Thutmose IV. The mummy resting at the bottom of the trough on a board. The mummy is well-preserved and bears in ink on the shroud, the prenomen of King Men-Kheperu-Re. Length 1m 69 Breadth at shoulders 0m 40.

2. Trough and lid mismatching. On the trough is the name of Ramesses III, which is one of the mummies found at Deir el Bahari and is in the Museum at Gizeh. The lid, marked for another coffin and washed yellow, bears the names of Seti II, but an hieratic addition gives us the pre-nomen of Amunhotep III. The mummy, well-preserved and covered with flowers, bears the same pre-nomen as Amunhotep III, as well as an indication of the name of Pinudjem, of which I have given previously the first letters.[13] Length 1m 58 Breadth at shoulders 0m 41.

3. Trough of wood without lid. This coffin is covered with a wash of yellow, in order to hide the original

---

13 The legend on the mummy said that in the Year 12, fourth month of winter, day six, the First Priest of Amun-Ra, Pinudjem, [Pinudjem I] wrapped the king Amunhotep.

decorations. The mummy is well-preserved, bearing on the chest the name of Seti II. Length 1m 62. Breadth at shoulders 0m 36.

4. Trough of wood without lid, belonging to Setnakhte. The mummy, having on the neck some stalks of an umbelliferous plant, bears the name of "Khou-n-Aten". Length 1m75 Breadth at shoulders 0m42.

5. Trough with lid. The whole thing was adzed in order to efface the name of the original owner. On the cover, the name of Siptah. The mummy, restored and rewrapped, bears on the legs the prenomen of the same king. Length 1m 63 Breadth at shoulders 0m 34.

6. The mummy lying on the bottom of the rectangular coffin. It had been stripped and thrown in, in an incomplete state. On the breast, a prenomen nearly effaced of which the forms and the disposition of the legible signs permit me to recognize the prenomen of Ramesses V. Length 1m77 Breadth at shoulders 0m36.

7. Lid lying on its face and taking the place of a coffin. Everywhere is the name and prenomen of Setnakhte. The mummy was stripped and the shroud which bore the name was removed. This mummy very much resembles that of Setnakhte.[14] 1m57 0m35.

---

14 Victor Loret had no sure way of knowing that this mummy was a woman. It was pronounced a female by Dr. Smith and is referred to as "Unknown Woman D". Why Loret said the mummy "*resembles that of Setnakhte*" is obscure, since he did not see a mummy named Setnakht in KV35 and no Setnakht was recovered from the Deir el

8. Trough and lid of wood painted black. On it the name of the First Prophet of Amun, first prophet of Thutmose III, Ra. On the lid, scratched and scraped, a cartouche with the prenomen of Ramesses VI. The mummy, of whom the head has been broken to pieces, doesn't bear a name. Impossible to measure.

9. Trough and lid of wood painted white. Name and prenomen of Ramesses IV. The mummy, very deteriorated, bears on a fragment of linen a name entirely effaced and impossible to read. 1m60 0m41.

Because of the positioning of the coffins in antiquity, the exploration of KV35 by Victor Loret would not be without its spatial difficulties. Loret wrote that, when he first examined the nine mummies, they were covered in the thick dust of the ages. *"The mummies were a uniform grey color. I leaned over the nearest coffin and blew on it to read the name. The gray tint was a layer of dust which flew away and let me read the name and prenomen of Ramesses IV..."*
    Surely Loret meant that he was able to read the cartouches on the coffin nearest to him in the beginning, but not the hieratic inscriptions on the shrouds, which later proved difficult to make out even under much more favorable and better-illuminated conditions. At that first moment in the side chamber, *"nine coffins laid on the*

Bahri cache. Perhaps he meant the face on the coffin. The mummy has no visible breasts and the genital area is missing, to all appearances. Smith measured the height of the body as being 1m 589 mill.

ground, six at the back, occupying all the space, three in the front, leaving to the right a small free space. There was only room in the length of the room for two coffins, in the width for six, so that the mummies touched at their head, shoulders and feet. Five coffins had lids, the other four were without. It was not for a moment possible to think of entering the room and looking at the coffins at closer quarters."

So here Loret admits that the containers and mummies had already been shifted into the next room before he even had a chance to blow the dust off all of them. Yet, in his notes, there does appear to be a kind of genealogical order to them, although it is not clear how the Frenchman now exactly remembered the sequence in which they had lain in the side-chamber, since he had not been able to walk among them in order to decipher their texts. From his own description of the mummies' proximity to one another, it becomes clear that the workmen, in these cramped quarters, had ample opportunity to create some sort of mix-up because they had first to remove the bodies closest to the free-space in the room. It is possible, therefore, that they were not able to duplicate an exact "line-up" in the adjacent *"grande salle"*. But perhaps they did.

Without a doubt, the most striking feature of Loret's description of the nine mummies is that he thought he distinguished the name of "Khou-n-aten", his reading of the signs of the name of the pharaoh of the 18th Dynasty, Akhenaten. Since he mentions this nomen in the same breath with a garland about the neck of this particular mummy, presumably he read this inscription on the mummy's outer wrapping, although Loret is vague about this. On the other hand, while he complains of other royal names as being barely legible, he does not make this comment about the name of Akhenaten that he saw in the dimly-lit tomb.

Once out of KV35, the mummies eventually underwent unwrapping and examination by Dr G. Elliot Smith. The mummy which Victor Loret had apparently judged to be Akhenaten was divested of its bandages on July 8, 1907, six years after it had been taken from the tomb. Smith says that Gaston Maspero, in his "Guide du Visiteur au Musee du Caire", made the notation: *"Mummy of the Pharaoh Meneptah, son and successor of Ramses II, found in the coffin of Setnakht. Monsieur Loret thought he recognized the mummy of ...Khouniatonou. M. Groff was the first to affirm that this was Menephtah, and the reading of the cartouche, traced in hieratic writing on the breast of the mummy, demonstrates the correctness of his opinion."*

Certainly, if the deceased found in the lid of the coffin of Setnakht was the one Loret assumed to be Akhenaten, Loret would have been very wrong, indeed. The mummy now known as Merneptah is not someone who would likely, judging by everything about him, have been a member of the Thutmosid Dynasty. Dr. Smith, who had already unwrapped Seti I and Ramesses II, found Merneptah to resemble these kings most remarkably. While describing the various aspects of the bandages of this corpse, Smith commented *"Not a fragment of writing, nor ornaments of any kind, were found on the mummy."* Presumably, Smith was not counting the inscription on the "breast", mentioned by Loret and Maspero.

Throughout his book, "The Royal Mummies", one can't help but notice that, in certain things, Smith usually defers to Maspero. Since the doctor was no Egyptologist, he had little choice. So it is noteworthy that, with regard to this hieratic writing, Smith has Maspero saying it existed, but never affirms that he saw it, himself. Dr. Smith did say that *the body is thickly encrusted with salt*. Was this the information that reinforced the identification of Merneptah who was, as Maspero puts it *...after a tradition of the Alexandrian epoch, the Pharaoh of the Exodus, the one who, it is said, perished in the Red Sea*? Indeed, the oldest theory of an actual Egyptologist about the Pharaoh of the Book of Exodus named Merneptah as the candidate.

William Groff did set forth his credible arguments for the reading "BA n ra", a short rendering of the prenomen of Merneptah, but there is still the enigma of why the other mummy, the putative Seti II, appears to be a most unlikely scion of the early Ramessids. Nevertheless, it is not the mummy we know as "Seti II" that Loret described as having umbelliferae at the neck or upon which he noticed the name of Akhenaten—but the one he indicates was lying next to it. Yet, if Seti II had been Akhenaten, there would have been a correct dynastic progression of the mummies lying in KV35—straight from Amunhotep II, in his stone sarcophagus, through Akhenaten.

Otherwise, if Seti II is really that ruler, then he would be, according to our understanding of the royal succession, out of order because he is followed by the mummy now considered to be Merneptah, who himself appears to be followed by Siptah[15] and then Ramesses V. If everyone is who the hieratic dockets say he is, or at least if what the early Egyptologists read there is correct, either a totally strict order was not followed in the positioning of the coffins by the ancient restorers—or Victor Loret could not recall the original order exactly. As of now, nothing can be concluded regarding why the purported Seti II looks so different from his predecessors. DNA testing of this mummy is certainly in order, however, in the hope of clearing up any doubts.

It has generally been taken for granted that Seti II was the same as Crown Prince Seti-Merneptah, son of King Merneptah. For some reason, however, this heir

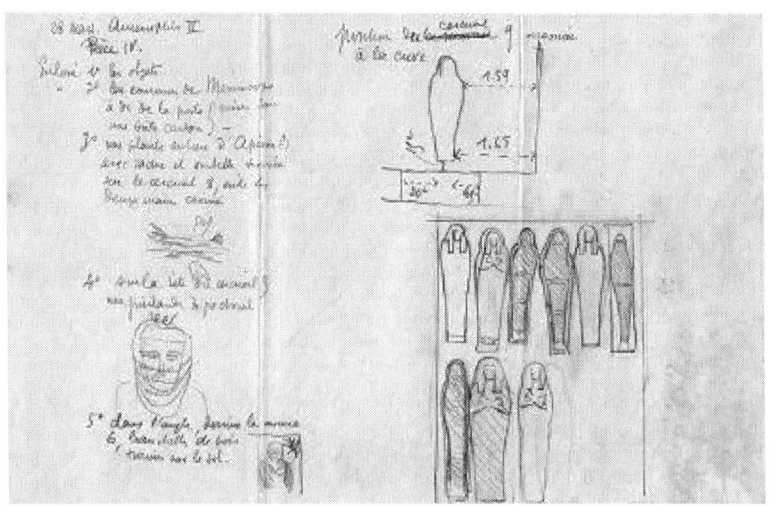

The notes of Loret

---

15 Userkheperure Seti II was a successor of Merneptah and Siptah apparently a succesor of Seti II.

39

decided to revert back to the "xprw" element in his prenomen that was used by the pharaohs of the 18th Dynasty. In his tomb, KV15, images such as the king standing on the back of a panther and as harpooner riding in a papyrus skiff, harked back to objects from the tomb of Tutankhamun.

Smith, examining the mummy known as Seti II, remarked: "*There is little resemblance to the other XIXth Dynasty pharaohs in Seti IInd's features, but they recall in a striking manner those of the XVIIIth Dynasty.*"

This statement is true to a remarkable degree. The mummy in question, pronounced by Dr. Smith to be young or middle-aged, has a pentagonoid cranium. No other royal mummy has a flatter skull except for the platycephalic Thutmose III. The pronounced Thutmosid over-bite of the mummy is certainly very much in evidence, and so is the under-slung jaw, quite long in this case. The nose is high-bridged but not especially lengthy. Is it possible that some descendant of the 18th Dynasty rulers managed to become king by virtue of his genealogy? King Horemheb claimed that Thutmose III was "the father of my fathers", even though there is nothing else linking him to that family—except that he was a powerful man during the reign of Tutankhamun.

To add to the mystery, the mummy known as Siptah has all the same cranio-facial characteristics as the above and his head very much resembles that of Tutankhamun when one compares their profiles in photos. Their wide crania also are close in measurement. While quite short, the young man called Siptah [who might have been merely half-grown, after all, as he came to the throne as a child] has a cranium that is somewhere in size between Seti II and Tutankhamun and the KV55 remains.

The embalming incisions of both Seti II and Siptah are sewn together with a thin strip of linen—but so is that of old Thuya, the mother of Queen Tiye. Like that of the Younger Lady of KV35, the mouth of Siptah was stuffed with very fine cloth. His face also suffered much the same ill treatment as hers. Smith wrote: *"The right cheek and front teeth had been badly broken by a blow long after the embalming process, and at the same time the lips and the whole right side of the cheek down to the chin had been broken away. This was done before the mummy was rewrapped, because the missing parts were not in the bandages. The ears were broken off."*

Because Akhenre Siptah[16] was not recognized by the following 20th Dynasty as a legitimate king, it is supposed he was not the son of the recognized Seti II. The theory is that his father was the likewise excoriated Amunmesse, a counter-king and rival of Seti II. Was Amunmesse a brother of Seti II that his son should so much resemble Seti? And who was Amunmesse? It took almost a century after his examination by Grafton Elliot Smith before it was realized that young Siptah had something else in common with the royals of the end of Dynasty 18. Siptah had a club foot and that was noted by Smith. One hundred years later, it was seen, via DNA

---

16 The boy-king had the same prenomen as the nomen "Akhenaten", except with "Re" instead of the Aten. He was later viewed as a female named "Alcandra" due to the way Akhenre was vocalized.

testing, that the royal family, starting with Amunhotep III, carried the gene that caused talipes equinovarus and that some of the women were badly deformed as a result.[7]

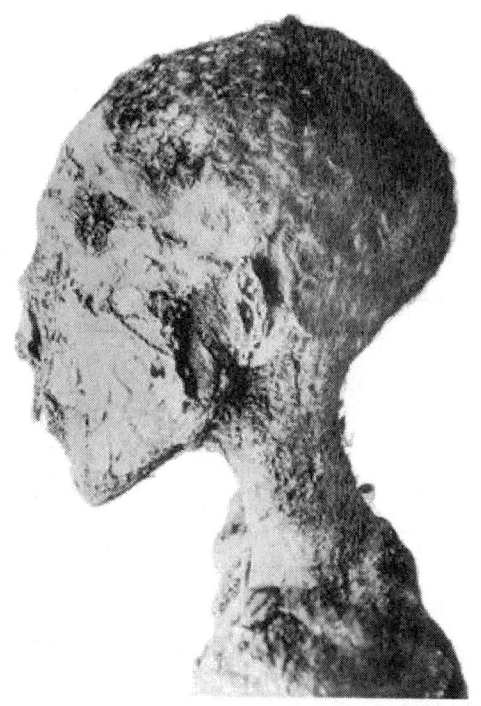

The head of Siptah, as seen in "The Royal Mummies".

There were high quality linen shirts found among the wrappings of Seti II, which were monogrammed for King Merneptah. These shirts could have been provided by the restoration party and this appears to have been the

---

17 Smith called Seti II and Siptah "*the feeble successors of Merneptah*".

case. More difficult to explain is a string of blue-glaze Eyes of Horus tied around the legs of the mummy and firmly embedded in the resinous mass, presumably applied during the original embalming. Since the Eye of Horus was thought to have healing or restorative qualities, perhaps this ruler had problems with his legs while alive and the amulets were intended to guarantee their sound use in the afterlife.

The embalming of the mummy generally conforms to the 18th Dynasty method and a large section of the individual's chest was hacked away by thieves in the same fashion as the three 18th Dynasty mummies on the floor of the "treasury". The strongest argument of all against Seti II being an 18th Dynasty mummy is that his face is covered with a layer of resinous paste, in the manner of Siptah and Ramesses III—although not nearly so thickly applied. The majority of the royal mummies of the 18th Dynasty have admirably preserved faces with the exception of Tutankhamun, the skin of his face being cracked, brittle and greyish from being treated with some compound. The body cavity of Siptah was stuffed with lichen, also something not usually noted about the mummies of Dynasty 18. However, both the corpses of the KV35YL and that of Seti II had been packed with *"pieces of linen soaked in a solution of resin, which set into a stone-like mass..."* Like that of the royal woman, the right arm of Seti II was *"separated from the body."*[18]

---

18 The detached right arm of a man was found inside the bandages of the KV35YL—probably the same arm that was tested for DNA chromosomes, resulting in this mummy being temporarily

Also significant is that, as of yet, we cannot prove that any of the identifications assigned to the royal mummies in the form of ancient dockets are in error. However, regarding the inscription on the shroud in which the mummy had been wrapped, Dr. Smith only comments: *"There was a faint traces of the name written* [in ink] *in hieratic on the front of this piece of linen."*

There has been no real tendency among Egyptologists to express any grave doubts about the later 19th Dynasty mummies, but further examination might prove interesting, nevertheless. Some 300 years before the Common Era there lived an Egyptian with the unusual name of Manetho, a man to whose writings I have given a great deal of attention. The history of Egypt that was Manetho's great work was largely lost, except as excerpts copied by Flavius Josephus. One of these extracts was a story now known as "The Tale of the Polluted Ones". Regarding it, Josephus had the sagacity to comment *"...So long as Manetho followed the ancient records, he did not stray far from the truth, but when he turned to unauthorized legends, he either combined them in an improbable form or else gave credence to certain prejudiced informants."*

What Manetho seems to have combined are the names "Amunhotep" and "Merneptah" in the form of a

---

declared by the Egyptians to be a male. The right forearm and hand of Seti II were missing during Smith's "autopsy", but were evidently recovered in the wrappings of Ramesses VI [Reeves,Wilkinson] **The Complete Valley of the Kings** [p. 165] Both of the arms of Seti II were separated from his body and he received *"numerous blows to the head with some sharp instrument"*—post mortem. [Smith]

44

king called "Amenophis". In the beginning of the tale, he seems to be writing about the former but, then, Amenophis abruptly appears to become the latter. The pharaoh of the story was driven from his throne by a dissident faction and fled south to the protection of the Viceroy of Kush. At the time, according to Manetho, Amenophis had a son *"Sethos also called Ramesses after his grandfather Ra[m]pses..."*, whose care he entrusted to a friend. When this boy grew up, he was able to help his father defeat the enemies and banish them from Egypt.

Most legends contain a kernel of truth, as difficult as that may be to detect at times. There may have been a connection between a pharaoh named Amunhotep and the end of Dynasty 19 of which we are unaware. An historian like Manetho was able to write the word "son" and it could have more than one nuance because, for the Egyptians, "son" had never had a single meaning. Just as their term for "father" could mean "ancestor", a "son" could be a descendant or, in the case of a king, a successor. Therefore, in ancient Egypt, it was possible for a man to be both the "son" and the "successor" of kings of two different dynasties, vindicating them both. Once, such a knotty state of affairs could never have been untangled but now it could be. Even a dead man can be connected to or separated from other dead men by virtue of what is known as "yDNA", that which men pass on to their sons in an unbroken chain until their line becomes extinct. That occurs only when there are no more males who bear that same yDNA.[19] Whether or not they know

---

19 Although, usually, it is interpreted more narrowly as meaning that the only surviving male in a certain family dies without producing a son.

if or how they are related does not matter—although nowadays one is able to find relatives via genetic testing. It is not at all unusual for men with different surnames to have the same yDNA due to a common ancestor. Surnames do not go back as far in time as DNA. They can have been acquired by several means and even subsequently changed.

And so, that may be why Seti II, despite his name, was placed next to the 18th Dynasty rulers in KV35. Because someone remembered his connection to them. Whether that be true or false can now be determined. We can find out if Seti II was really a son of King Merneptah or some descendant of Amunhotep III,[20] who had managed to seize power during a period of "throne wars".

In my younger years, I knew that the royals were kept in Room 52 of the Cairo Egyptian Museum. By the 90's, when I began to do more thinking about KV35, it began to seem odd to me that the coffin-less trio, Elder Lady, Younger Lady, and Young Prince, remained walled-up inside the "treasury" of the tomb where no one could see them. I found them tremendously intriguing and couldn't comprehend why they were so ignored. Although many of the other royal mummies had been subjected to x-ray since their scrutiny by Dr. Smith, the ashlar wall concealing the two women and the boy remained intact. After I had written my 1999 paper, a

---

20 Or some other 18th Dynasty pharaoh. If Horemheb was telling the truth when he said that Thutmose III was his ancestor, then the Thutmosid line did not die out with Tutankhamun, as is often assumed.

German television production company got in touch with me via email, saying they had received permission from the Egyptian authorities to film the three mummies. My paper had inspired the endeavor and they thought I might be interested. I certainly was, but never did manage to see the resulting documentary. After the Germans had done their filming, the wall went up again.

I was also contacted by a representative of Brando Quilici, another producer of documentaries, asking for an on-camera interview about Nefertiti. This was, I believe, in 2005. My answer was that, until the KV35YL had her DNA extracted and tested, along with others of Dynasty 18, there was no point in saying anything more about her. I had made my arguments for the identification in my online paper and had nothing further to add. Talk was cheap. Besides, the equation of the Younger Lady with Nefertiti had already been generally rejected. What was needed was proof, a connection.

A couple of years earlier, the Egyptians had pronounced the KV35YL a male, having done what is known as a "quick test" for gender, utilizing a fragment of bone, as they specified in a report that used to be online. I never believed for a second that the mummy was that of a man because I knew what Prof. Smith had written about the treatment of the mummy's genitals—same as that of the Elder Lady. I also knew that Zahi Hawass, the Egyptologist in charge of antiquities at the time, would not have permitted bone to be removed from the mummy, itself. One of the loose arms, wrapped with the KV35YL, had to be involved and I said so several times on the Internet, now facing further derision from those who insisted that I give up my theory about her being Queen Nefertiti. The announcement coming out of Egypt had no effect on my thinking whatsoever.

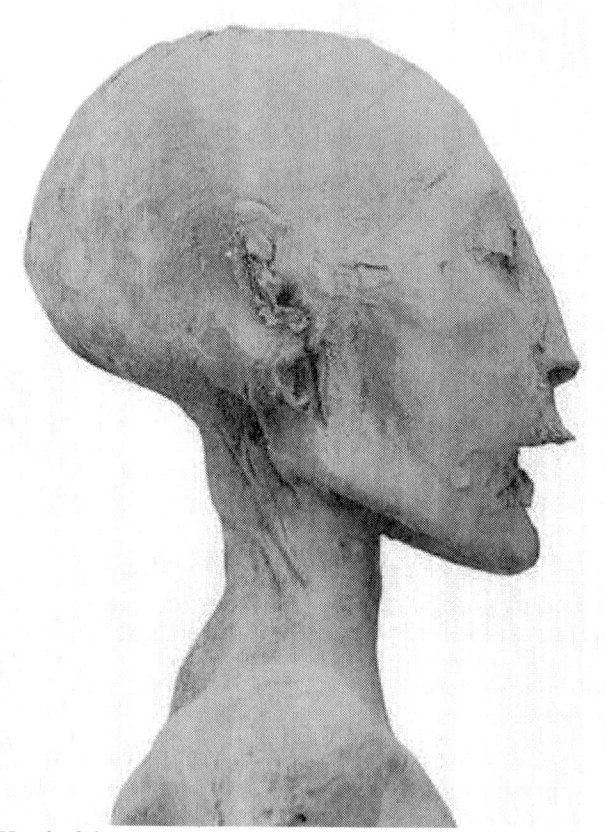

Head of the Younger Lady as seen in "The Royal Mummies"

Chapter Two

MYSTERIOUS MUMMIES

One hates to make posthumous accusations, but that Gaston Maspero could be virtually blind when it came to certain mummies and their identities has been proved. The director of the Boulaq Museum once argued that a certain lady from the Deir el Bahri cache was not who she was advertised to be, even though her shroud clearly declared her *"The king's daughter and king's sister, Meryetamun, may she live"*. Maspero, in 1886, saw her as a mummy of the Middle Kingdom and a replacement for the original Meryetamun,[21] a notion with which G. Elliot Smith, to his credit, for once did not

---

21 Meryetamun was surely a common name in the era of the 18ᵗʰ Dynasty. Thutmose III had more than one daughter called Meryetamun. Another Meryetamun was found inside a most beautifully carved coffin in a tomb [TT358] beneath the first terrace of Hatshepsut's mortuary temple. This one was a sister of Amunhotep I, although Herbert Winlock, the lady's discoverer, had concluded her to be one of the daughters of Thutmose.

concur.

Nevertheless, this incident demonstrates that Maspero was not above disregarding evidence, if he so chose. It is already known that Gaston Maspero wanted so badly to have a complete set of early Thutmosid kings that he and Smith, both, evidently overlooked factors concerning "Thutmose I" that would definitely not have argued in favor of this identification. [The mummy is not a king; its arms are not crossed.] I would also suggest that, by the time of the publication of "The Royal Mummies", Maspero was quite convinced that the remains found in KV55, the so-called "Tomb of Queen Tiye", were those of Akhenaten.[22] Here he was on much surer ground. In describing these KV55 remains, Dr. Smith wrote: "*The mummy under consideration, however, was not rewrapped. It had not been plundered, but was found in its original wrappings, upon which were the gold bands bearing the name of Khouniatonou. It is hardly credible that the embalmers of the Pharaoh's mummy would have put some other body in place of it. Thus we have the most positive evidence that these bones are the remains of Khouniatonou.*"

Arthur Weigall, who was, for a time, Chief Inspector of Antiquities for Upper Egypt,[23] wrote: "*The body was lying in a coffin inscribed with Akhnaton's name; it was bound with ribbons inscribed with his name; it had the physical characteristics of the portraits of Akhnaton; it had the idiosyncrasies of a religious reformer such as he was; it was that of a man of*

---

22 Discovered by Theodore Davis in 1907.
23 1905 through 1911.

Akhnaton's age as deduced from the monuments; it lay in the tomb of Akhnaton's mother;[24] *those who erased the names must have thought it to be Akhnaton's body; unless one supposes an utter chaos of cross-purposes in their actions; and, finally, there is nobody else who, with any degree of probability, it could possibly be."*

Since 1912 some doubts have overshadowed this conclusion—and that is an understatement. Those gold bands, mentioned by Smith, [they being the "ribbons" of Weigall] like the shirts found on the mummy of Seti II, mysteriously disappeared from the Boulaq museum.

Theodore Davis, a very wealthy American, who was the sponsor of the excavation of KV55 in 1907, was very disappointed that a smallish mummy, found in a rather magnificent, gold-lined, wooden coffin, crumbled into dust and mere skeleton when human hands touched it for the first time in many centuries. Water had penetrated the tomb and the resulting damp had played havoc with everything inside KV55 not made from a durable material.

Arthur Weigall conveyed the KV55 bones to Dr. Smith for evaluation, who wrote him back, saying *"Are you sure that the bones you sent to me are those which were found in the tomb? Instead of an old woman, you have sent me those of a young man. Surely there is some mistake."*

G. Elliot Smith's examination was subsequently

---

24 The undecorated KV55 was, in those days, thought to be the tomb of Queen Tiye [and this was the title of a book published about it] because the remains of her gold-covered funerary shrine were inside it. Theodore Davis went to his own grave convinced this was the queen's tomb and that the body therein was that of Tiye.

51

corroborated by others over the years and, within my lifetime, no expert has ever reached any other conclusion. But this was the only thing about the dead ancient Egyptian that remained free from controversy.

People believed it was fortunate that several busts of Queen Nefertiti had survived the ravages of time, the supreme one, of course, being in the Berlin Egyptian Museum. Yet, by the middle of the 20th Century, few considered that there was such a thing as the mummy of Akhenaten—or that of Nefertiti.

The pharaoh had decreed on stone that he and his family be buried in the royal tomb at Amarna. That was found to be empty. Not even Princess Meketaten, whose "wake" was depicted therein, remained inside to prove that it had really happened. [25] Since Akhenaten and his heresy were so reviled by the next couple of dynasties, it began to be taken for granted that his mummy and those of his wife and children were destroyed.

Those successors, Smenkhkare, Tutankhamun, Ay, and Horemheb were not considered the sons of Akhenaten and owed him nothing. Tut probably never even knew him. Whatever daughters of Akhenaten survived him were perhaps powerless to do anything to salvage the memories or corpses of their mother and father or their sisters. No one suspected any filial piety on the part of Tutankhamun at all. Akhetaten had been abandoned to the jackals and serpents, and even Queen Ankhesenamun, the wife of Tutankhamun and daughter of Akhenaten and Nefertiti, had left there early in her

---

25 However, fragments of a red granite sarcophagus belonging to the princess were found.

husband's reign. General Horemheb, once he became pharaoh, demolished the stone buildings and the talatat blocks were reused elsewhere. Nobody cared about the ruins except as a spot for scavenging until the discipline of Egyptology came into being.

Egyptologists Nicholas Reeves and Geoffrey Martin believed that a tomb for Nefertiti could possibly be found in the Valley of the Kings, but their search for that, begun in 1998, was interrupted by a situation in Egypt that involved a confusing mixture of chauvinism, legalities, and ego—none of which could be attributed to Reeves and Martin.

Even prior to 1999, I had written a paper proposing that the mummy known as the Younger Lady from KV35 could be Nefertiti. I sent it to Dennis Forbes, the editor of **Kmt**, a popular magazine about ancient Egypt—but Forbes never responded with a yes or a no. Perhaps it had something to do with his belief that this was the mummy of Sitamun—but I found it incredible that the editor would fail to think that his readers would be interested in a plausible theory regarding Nefertiti. Although proof was lacking, there was certainly a fair amount of compelling evidence. Finally, I decided just to place the same observations on my website, sponsored by Geocities. I also compared the profile views of the head of the mummy and the most famous bust of the queen, demonstrating that with images. The piece proved the most popular one I had online by far. [By July 4, 2003, there had been 38,715 views.] It still exists on Oocities [Geocities having become defunct] and it looks like this:

53

DO WE HAVE THE MUMMY OF NEFERTITI?

By Marianne Luban ©1999

 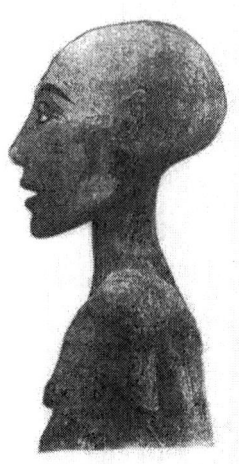

Limestone bust of Nefertiti, Berlin Museum

Unidentified female mummy from
KV35, dimensions slightly restored

When Victor Loret, a French Egyptologist, found a trio of denuded, unidentified mummies lying side-by-side on the floor of the tomb of Amenhotep II (designated "King's Valley, No. 35"), he described them as an older woman, a little prince and a young man[26]. Later, it was

---

26 A total of seventeen mummies, both labeled and anonymous, were discovered in KV35, among them great kings of the 18th, 19th, and 20th Dynasties.

determined that the "young man" was, in fact, a woman, her baldness having confused even a Frenchman like Loret:

"*The last corpse nearest the wall seemed to be that of a man. His head was shaved but a wig lay on the ground not far from him. The face of this person displayed something horrible and something droll at the same time. The mouth, running obliquely from one side nearly to the middle of the cheek, bit a pad of linen whose two ends hung from the corner of the lips. The half-closed eyes had a strange expression; he could have died choking on a gag but he looked like a young, playful cat with a piece of cloth. Death, which had respected the severe beauty of the woman and the impish grace of the boy, had turned in derision and amused itself with the countenance of the man.*"[27]

The female mummy who had managed to retain a "severe beauty", has, in recent years, been identified as Queen Tiye, the Chief Wife of the pharaoh, Amenhotep III. A sample of hair from the head of this mummy was compared with a lock of hair within a small case discovered in the tomb of Tutankhamun. The two samples were deemed a perfect match. However, since the identification has been challenged for several reasons, this mummy is still mostly known to Egyptologists as the " Elder Lady".[28] The young prince

---

27 Romer, John, **Valley of the Kings** (New York, 1981).
28 The identity is based, not on hair, but on the inscription of Queen Tiye's name and titles on the mummiform case. To suppose that the

has not been identified, although I think he bears a considerable facial resemblance to the latter and may be Prince Thutmose, the eldest son of Amenhotep III, who died at an undetermined age and was succeeded as heir by his brother, who later became Amenhotep IV or Akhenaten.

Akhenaten was the 18th Dynasty king who established the monotheistic worship of the sun-god, the Aten, and built his capital, Akhetaten, ("The Horizon of the Aten") in the desert on the site now known as Tel el Amarna. He abolished the worship of the gods of Egypt and, as a result, the temples fell into neglect and the priests lost much of their wealth and power. Such cultural activities and scholarship that would normally have been centered around the temples went into a decline and the ordinary people who made a living supplying these edifices of the gods with commodities of every sort, also felt the crunch.

In addition, Akhenaten's effectiveness as administrator of the Egyptian Empire, the legacy of his warlike ancestors, is in considerable doubt. As a result, it was unlikely that this pharaoh's iconoclastic and eccentric seventeen-year

---

mummy is Queen Tiye is to suppose that the hair in the case actually came from the head of that great lady. Since the hair of the mummy is still dark brown and without gray and the teeth only moderately worn, it has been questioned that this can be Tiye, who, according to the generally accepted understanding of her history, must have been quite an elderly lady when she died. However, that is only if one assumes a short or no co-regency between her son, Akhenaten, and his father, Amenhotep III. As I believe, judging from facial characteristics, that this mummy is, indeed, Queen Tiye, I would have to find it a powerful argument for a lengthy co-regency . The late Cyril Aldred proposed it was as long as twelve years.

reign was popular with anybody except his faithful followers at Akhetaten.[29] The foremost among these was Akhenaten's beautiful queen, Nefertiti.

The exact age of the mummy, the man- who -proved -a - female, cannot be positively fixed, but the body is not entirely without clues as regards its place in the chronology of ancient Egypt. The process by which this woman was mummified seems to date her to the latter part of the 18th Dynasty.[30] The unusual shape of her skull puts her in the Amarna period, where this type of cranial formation was either artificially fostered or a genetic condition. The skull of the "Younger Lady" from KV35 corresponds closely to those of Tutankhamun and the mummy of a young individual from KV55, (the so called "tomb of Queen Tiye"). It is also like the heads of the Amarna princesses, as seen in the art of that era. And, not least, there may have been a skull shaped like that of the "Younger Lady" under the tall, blue crown of Queen Nefertiti, the Great Royal Wife of Akhenaten.

Clearly, the mummy has suffered from the cavalier attentions of ancient plunderers. Like the other two mummies with which it was found, its skull is pierced with a large hole and the chest has been hacked away.[31] Worse yet, the face, which would have otherwise been excellently preserved, has been cruelly mutilated, its

---

29 The possibility exists that, although the temples of the old gods were abandoned, the new religion did not actually catch on in Egypt anywhere except at Akhetaten, the royal city.

30 Smith, G. Elliot, **The Royal Mummies** (Cairo, 1912).

31 In order to get at the "heart scarab", which in the case of a royal mummy, could be made of gold and other valuable materials.

mouth and cheek no more than a gaping hole. On the other hand, the mummy seems to have suffered from an unjust lack of attention from modern investigators. I suppose it has been difficult to imagine this hairless, battered corpse as having once been a beautiful anybody, much less an Egyptian queen of legendary loveliness.

Some have postulated that this might be the body of Sitamun, a daughter of Amenhotep III, whom he also seems to have married and who would perhaps have been interred with him and her mother, the chief queen. Sitamun, it is true, would have been considered of a very high status, and it is far more likely that a king's wife would have been taken to the two royal caches by the priests of the re-burial commissions than a mere king's daughter.[32] At this writing, I do not know whether a DNA sample has been taken from the mummy in question for comparison with that of the other 18th Dynasty royals.[33]

I think it is safe to assume that, were the mummy of Queen Nefertiti to be discovered, it would probably have

32 The priests of the re-burial commission, who transported the mummies to the Deir el Bahari cache and KV35, appear to have been quite selective in whom they chose for these repositories. Because of their polygamous habits, the pharaohs presumably had plenty of daughters, yet few that were not queens found their way into the two collections of royal mummies. Likewise the male progeny. I know of only two example of mummies of little princes with "the Horus-lock" on their otherwise shaved heads. The one in the tomb of Thutmose IV was not even removed for safe-keeping in KV35 with his father, but was found propped up against a wall of his father's own tomb (KV43) by Howard Carter in 1903.

33 Professor Scott Woodward of Brigham Young University, a microbiologist, has taken samples of several of the mummies. I eagerly await his findings.

little remaining of the exquisite beauty of the famous bust in the Berlin Museum. Yet, in my view, the bone-structures of the "Younger Lady" and Nefertiti, as immortalized in stone, are strikingly similar. Each has a slender neck of extraordinary length and a strong, but very beautiful jawline. Seen from the front, the mummy's jaw appears quite square in the manner of the likeness of Nefertiti. Also very alike are the noses that descend in almost an unbroken line from the brow and the angle of the eye sockets in relation to the nose. The eyelids are long in both cases.

The mouth of the mummy is now impossible to determine, so I gave her the full lips of the sculpture in my restoration of the mummy's profile and these seem to fit quite well with the rest of the face. Unlike the figures of her mother-in-law, Tiye, Nefertiti does not give the impression, in her portraits, of being an especially diminutive woman and sometimes she is shown as being nearly on a level with the king. While the mummy of the "Elder Lady" measures only 1.455 metres, the younger one is 1.580 metres in height.[34] Since the putative mummy of Tiye's husband, Amenhotep III, is only 1.561 metres, I think we may safely conclude that, with such parents, Akhenaten was lucky to have been 1.580 metres tall, himself.[35] The chances of Sitamun, his sister, ever

34 Somewhat over 5 feet 2 inches.
35 Amenhotep III is the shortest of the pharaohs whose mummies we have—except the mummy of Thutmose I, measuring only 1.545 metres. However, I believe this mummy is most certainly that of a woman and not a man. See my article "Is the Mummy Thutmose I Really Hatshepsut", Discussions In Egyptology, Vol. 42, InScription, Issue 4, Autumn, both 1998, and Kemet, Spring, 1999.

achieving this "height" are even less.

There is little doubt in my mind that, in order to facilitate the wearing of Nefertiti's famous unique crown, a tight, narrow head-dress, the skull would be shaved like that of the mummy of the "Younger Lady" from KV35. Moreover, the one preserved ear of the mummy appears to be "double-pierced", a feature I have observed in more than one of Nefertiti's probable portraits.[36] As an experiment, I took a full-size photo of a life-size bust of what is thought to be a young Nefertiti and decided to do some measuring to determine if its dimensions co-respond to the facial measurements of the mummy as obtained by G. Elliot Smith, the professor of anatomy who wrote the invaluable book, "The Royal Mummies" (1912).

Smith obtained 94mm as a "minimal frontal breadth" on the mummy. This I understand to be the distance of the forehead between the two frontal lobes. These are very clearly marked on the bust and, measuring between them, I got 94-95mm, as well. Smith gave 112 mm as an "auricular height". I don't know exactly how he measured the height of the ears, but when I put my tape measure at the base of the chin of the bust, 112 mm was the point where the ear is attached to the head in its upper part. As a "total facial height", Smith got 119 mm. I would say this is not an easy thing to measure on a bald-headed

---

36 A yellow quartzite head, Aegyptisches Museum, Berlin, and the Wilbour Plaque, which can be viewed on pages 72 and 90, respectively, of the Metropolitan Museum's **The Royal Women of Amarna**, which will be further used as an illustration source for the works of art discussed in this article.

mummy, but perhaps Smith saw the shadow of a hairline. The bust I measured has no hairline because the queen is wearing a diadem (it being a "composite statue" upon which a crown, presumably the tall blue one, would be added of a different material).

However, placing my tape at the tip of the chin, I see that 119 mm is a very reasonable facial height for this bust and could have been where the natural hairline began. The only thing left that I was able to measure was the nose. Smith got 56mm for the nasal height and, yes, if I place my tape at the end of the nose of the bust I get 56mm up to the spot where the nasal bridge begins—the part that is supposed to jut out from the brow. I say "supposed to" because this would not be very pronounced in either the case of the mummy or of the bust. In most of her busts Nefertiti seems to have almost a "Grecian profile". Since this is very noticeable on the mummy, it is one of the reasons I think she may be Nefertiti. Unlike Smith, I cannot get a nasal breadth of 25mm. This is simply too narrow and is probably due to the desiccation of the cartilage that one sees on all Egyptian mummies. The marks for "double-piercing" of the ears are very evident on the bust I measured, although the holes were never drilled, the piece having been left unfinished.

In one photograph, the "Elder Lady", the prince and the younger female (if, in fact, she is actually younger)[37] all

---

37 We have no real idea at all how old Tiye was when she died, although the great Amarna scholar, Cyril Aldred, wrote that, historically, fifty years had to go by between her marriage to the king and her death. The "Elder lady" is hard to pinpoint as well. Because of her hair and other considerations, she has been given the round

seem to be arranged en famille, candles burning at their heads. I believe that they were found together is no accidental grouping and that the ancient restorers of the royal mummies may have understood that this trio was closely related. While it is true that the mummy's left arm is not raised in the queenly attitude, such as is that of "The Elder Lady", this does not necessarily disqualify her from being a king's wife in the unconventional and chaotic Amarna era. In fact, the right arm of the corpse is broken off above the elbow and a right arm that appears to have been flexed was discovered nearby in the chamber of the tomb where these mummies rested.

We have found no other female royal mummies with a raised right arm, but this anomaly can possibly be explained by Nefertiti's special status, which will be addressed herein: Nefertiti, it is believed by many, suddenly disappears from the iconography and textual records in about Year 13 of the rule of her husband, King Akhenaten. Since there are no reliefs showing her funeral, it has been assumed that she fell from favor for some reason and was supplanted by her own daughter, dying in a state of disgrace. In contradiction of this theory, that Nefertiti was given a queenly burial could be assumed because pieces of an ushabti figure bearing her name has been found. In fact, a reconstruction of it from

---

number of forty, (although Wente and Harris in their **X-ray Atlas of the Royal Mummies** gave her, on the basis of forensic examinations, a minimum age of 25 and a maximum of 35) a rather problematic figure to adjust to the chronology of the life of Queen Tiye, the mother of the heretic pharaoh, Akhenaten--unless she was a mere toddler upon her marriage. However, age estimates of the mummies have always tended to be on the conservative or low side

portions in the Louvre and Brooklyn Museums[38] bears the inscription "Great Heiress of the Palace, praised of the King of Upper and Lower Egypt (Akhenaten?)...Great Royal Wife, Neferneferuaten, Nefertiti, given life forever." Still, as we know tombs were prepared far in advance of a person's demise, this broken ushabti does not guarantee us much information about Nefertiti's ultimate position within the royal circle.

No one knows how old Nefertiti was when she died or exactly where she was (originally) buried. Even though she was a mother at least six times, giving birth to six princesses with whom she is often shown, she may have begun her child-bearing very early and been no more than thirty when her eldest daughter was fifteen. However, there is no proof that Queen Nefertiti died a young woman and there is also no conclusive proof that the mummy in KV35 is particularly young. The third molars of the mummy are reported not to have erupted, a normal indication of youth, but wisdom teeth do not erupt in all people. At this point we will examine the part that Nefertiti may have played in the reign of her husband, and its aftermath, and the work of art, so different from the world-famous bust of the queen, that most belies Nefertiti having disappeared around Year 13. This is a limestone statue of the aging beauty, also in the

---

38 Depicted in Volume One Depicted in Volume One (page 78) of the **Amarna Letters** published by KMT Communications, San Francisco. Some have seen this ushabti as being the proof that Nefertiti predeceased Akhenaten. Even if Nefertiti died in the reign of a later pharaoh, her old title may have been restored to her but the crook and flail added to her burial equipment to signify she had once been a co-regent or a "pharaoh" in her own right.

Agyptisches Museum, Berlin.[39]

In this sculpture Nefertiti is draped in a transparent, open robe that does not conceal her breasts in any way. On her head, instead of a tall, blue crown, she wears a rounded, blue helmet-like hat. It is quite clear that the figure of the queen has succumbed to the pull of gravity and the effects of numerous pregnancies. Her lovely face is actually ravaged—much older than it looks in any other portrait of Nefertiti of which I am aware. The point here is time, which not only destroys beauty but is the stuff of which chronologies are made. In this statuette Nefertiti, unless she was extremely ill when it was executed (her body certainly doesn't appear wasted) must have been a bare minimum of thirty years old.

Yet, as was mentioned, the conventional wisdom has pronounced that Nefertiti died or disappeared after Year 13 of Akhenaten. What are the mathematics involved here? Let us suppose that Akhenaten became co-regent with Amenhotep III at a minimum of age sixteen, a man in oriental terms, his own highest attested regnal year being 17. Just when he became sole king cannot be known with accuracy but, thirteen years later, Akhenaten would be twenty-nine. Indeed, Nefertiti, in her last portraits, looks this age—at very least—and may have even been between thirty and forty.[40]

---

39 Pages 77 through 79 Pages, **The Royal Women of Amarna.**

40 In her **The Royal Women of Amarna**, Dorothea Arnold takes the position that Nefertiti, as co-ruler with Akhenaten, assumed the status of "wise woman", vacated by the deceased Queen Tiye and is therefore prematurely aged in her portraits. I do not agree, as I cannot imagine the circumstances compelling enough to cause any woman,

Sometime after Year 13, Nefertiti was replaced as Great Royal Wife by her own daughter, Meritaten.[41] Donald Redford writes: "*In even the earliest reliefs Nefertiti is very often accompanied by a little daughter who follows behind her, clad like her mother and shaking the sistrum...If Meritaten was already a toddler in the second year of the reign, when the talatat structures began to arise, she can scarcely have been born later than the earliest months of her father's occupancy of the throne.*" [42]

By this reasoning, Meritaten was barely past reaching puberty in Year 13, hardly a rival to supplant a renowned beauty still possibly under the age of thirty who had been greatly loved by her husband, to all appearances. A tomb painting depicting the "great durbar" of the previous year shows the royal couple affectionately holding hands. Was Nefertiti perhaps dead within the next twelve months? But if Nefertiti had not died but had fallen out of favor by Year 13 and was yet a young woman of, say, twenty-eight or twenty-nine—why are there still portraits being commissioned of her in middle age with the uraeus on her brow?

The obvious answer is that the queen did not die young,

much less a celebrated beauty, to allow herself to be shown much older than in reality in any portrait, official or private.

41 James Allen, in "Two Altered Inscriptions of the Late Amarna Period" (JARCE XXV, 1988), argues that "*Meritaten's promotion to Chief Queen probably did not occur until after Akhenaten's Year 17*", and goes on to say that "*there is evidence both for the existence of Nefertiti as queen sometime after Year 17 and for the appearance of Neferneferuaten even later.*"

42 Redford, Donald B., **Akhenaten, the Heretic King** (New Jersey, 1984)

nor was she disgraced or supplanted in favor of another. If anything, the status of Nefertiti was elevated after Year 13 and that of her daughter, Meritaten, for the same reason,[43] a theory that increasingly gains support. In fact, it is very likely that Akhenaten declared Nefertiti his co-regent, styled "Ankhkheperure Neferneferuaten",[44] and that the khepresh-crowned individual who is probably seated next to him in the Stele of Pasi, whom he chucks under the chin and who does seem to have the lithe body of a woman, is not a young man named "Smenkhkare" after all.

Dr. James P. Allen, curator of the Egyptian department of the Metropolitan Museum of Art, New York, convinced me, with his article entitled "Akhenaten's Mystery Co-regent and Successor",[45] that the evidence for Nefertiti as co-regent and perhaps subsequent sole "king" exists for those whose minds are open to the notion.

Arguments offered by Julia Samson, following those of J.R. Harris, in her "Nefertiti and Cleopatra"[46] are compelling, as well. Earl L. Ertman, in his article "Is There Visual Evidence For A 'King' Nefertiti",[47] sums it

---

43 In the article quoted above, James Allen expresses the idea that the writing of Meritaten's name on the "Coregency Stela" represents "a stage between that of King's Daughter (without cartouche) and Chief Queen".

44 Attestations of this prenomen exist as "Ankhetkheperure", using the feminine form.

45 KMT, **Amarna Letters**, Vol. One, Fall 1991.

46 Samson, Julia, **Nefertiti and Cleopatra, Queen-Monarchs of Ancient Egypt** (London, 1997)

47 KMT, **Amarna Letters**, Vol. Two, Fall 1992.

up: "*The visual and textual evidence continues to mount that Neferneferuaten Nefertiti was co-ruler with her husband throughout much of his reign, performing duties and responsibilities of a king, if not actually holding the title. Her regalia and depicted actions suggest that she operated as co-king prior to Akhenaten's final years. Whether she ruled only while her husband was alive or also, in fact, succeeded him as sole ruler is still being reviewed and debated.*"

In my view Nefertiti was the co-regent of Akhenaten, but it was one of her older daughters who eventually became a"woman-king"called "Ankhkheperure Neferneferuaten", there being possibly three persons with the prenomen "Ankhkheperure" before the reign of Horemheb.

Why would an Egyptian king bestow so much simultaneous power and responsibility upon his own wife? The most logical answer would be that Akhenaten was a sick man and trusted only one individual implicitly—Nefertiti. It would also seem that the pharaoh, at least in Year 13, had no son that was even close to manhood because such an heir would have been the first choice to fill the role of "junior partner". Perhaps there were small sons or even the hope of an heir in Year 13. Whatever the situation was in this department, it is quite certain that the king's eldest daughter, Princess Meritaten, was ultimately given the title of Chief Wife and even foreign rulers seem to understand she is the mistress of Akhenaten's household. Meritaten perhaps gives birth to a little daughter, named after herself—although some have claimed the child as being that of Kiya, a lesser wife of Akhenaten. Regardless, Meritaten becomes a queen with a proper cartouche. Is it because she is the wife of Smenkhkare, the new co-king of the conventional wisdom—or is it due to the fact that the former Chief Wife is now the co-regent and has rejected this title in the manner of other "woman kings" before and after her?[48] We shall probably never know the answer to this puzzle or if Meritaten's father, sometime after Year 13, actually cohabited with her as a true wife or if her title was merely an honorary one at this point.

I am not one of those, like Samson, who is willing to completely dispense with the shadowy individual called "Smenkhkare" as a male. I believe there could have been a certain young man named Smenkhkare married to Akhenaten's eldest daughter, Meritaten, who became pharaoh for an instant, and that it may have been some of his funerary equipment that was altered for Tutankhamun. How to fit Smenkhkare into this theory of Nefertiti as co-regent with Akhenaten is problematic. However, since his reign lasted no longer than a year, it would not offend reason to postulate that this prince (perhaps a son of Amenhotep III by a minor queen) succeeded his half-brother, Akhenaten, and even adopted the same prenomen of "Ankhkheperure" so as to smooth over the traces that there ever was a female co-regent in the interim.

Of course, there are those who take the opposite view,

---

48 For example, both Hatshepsut of the 18th Dynasty and Tawosret of the 19th were once styled Great Royal Wife, but both relinquished this title upon becoming regents for their young princes.

steadfastly maintaining that there was only one "Ankhkheperure", the young man otherwise known as "Smenkhkare". Aidan Dodson, for example, has attempted to demonstrate a progression of this male co-regent's loyalty to the senior king by the changes in the inscriptions of a set of canopic coffinettes, which were ultimately used by Tutankhamun.[49] Dodson's theories in this area don't make much sense to me even though I am not able to dispute his epigraphic conclusions. I would tend to think that if Smenkhkare were a co-regent of Akhenaten and he wanted to mollify or please the heretic, he would probably have gotten some new coffinettes for his viscera that didn't display any of the traditional and taboo gods of Egypt or feature an emblem of Nekhbet, that great vulture goddess, smack in the center of his forehead. Are we to believe the co-regent sat in state with double emblems on his brow while Akhenaten contented himself merely with one—the cobra?

It appears to me that if young Smenkhkare wanted to show the "progress" he was making in currying favor with Akhenaten, he could have "re-worked" a lot more on these coffinettes than a few cartouches! ! So, somehow, it seems more logical to me to believe that those canopic coffinettes were *never* fashioned or modified during the sway of Akhenaten for anyone in a subordinate position to him and whom he ostensibly trusted to help him carry out his policies but by individuals who sat on the throne *after* Akhenaten was gone, even so they wanted to be

---

49 "King's Valley Tomb 55 and the Fates of the Amarna Kings", KMT's **Amarna Letters**, Vol. 3.

associated, nominally, with the latter.

In the twelfth year of his rule the pharaoh, Akhenaten, had at least one lovely wife and six growing daughters. This family unit is portrayed in the tomb of an official, Meryre II, with the king and queen perpetuating the artistic innovations of this regime by showing their affection for one another. Before two more years had passed, tragedy evidently struck. Perhaps it was due to a plague that may have eventually decimated the royal house, but there is no doubt that, by Year 14, Akhenaten's second daughter, the Princess Meketaten, was dead. We see her laid out in scenes in the Royal Tomb at Amarna, mourned by her distraught parents and the entire court. Most interestingly, these depictions also contain the figure of an infant, held in the arms of a nurse.[50] That the child is a male, perhaps the long-awaited heir, is indicated by the great deference shown to him with fan-bearers hovering in attendance lest strong light, heat or insects threaten this precious individual. Pestilence or no, the tiny, nameless person tantalizingly inserted into these scenes does likely survive and in due course becomes the pharaoh Tutankhamun, the most famous king of Egypt ever.

As it happens, the great posthumous renown of Tutankhamun is the only sure thing in all of this, for the period in which he was born, known to Egyptologists as

---

50 The French scholar, Marc Gabolde, has published a 300 page study of the period from year 12 of Akhenaten to the accession of Tutankhamun, **D'Akhenaton a Toutankhamon** (Paris, 1998). He cites the remnants of textual evidence that the child depicted in the scenes is born of Nefertiti, the Chief Wife of Akhenaten

the "Amarna Era", is shrouded with a figurative mist that shifts now and then but never lifts enough for scholars to get a firm grasp of the events of the time. In fact, the Amarna Era is highly vexatious to many scholars because it presents itself as a bundle with "loose ends" of which it is difficult to make a neat parcel. Theories have abounded nevertheless and many of them appear to be earnest efforts to render the events of this particular time as "normal" as possible, even harmonious, with a smooth succession from one king to the next. Yet it is my belief that the Amarna Era and its aftermath was far more chaotic and unusual than has been heretofore supposed. That is, supposed in modern times, because the ancient writers have certainly offered hints of the irregularities to which I refer, most of which have not been taken seriously by Amarna experts.

In his Year 17 Akhenaten apparently died, but there are indications that perhaps he was forced from his throne. At any rate, he disappears from the record. Even though Nefertiti may have been her husband's choice for a co-regent, it is doubtful that, after Akhenaten had passed from the scene, that she would have had any legal rights to the throne with grown daughters of the king being present.

Perhaps someday we shall know in whose reign Nefertiti actually died. Geoffrey Martin and Nicholas Reeves are searching for her tomb, but somehow I doubt they will discover her mummy in it. Regardless, we have no conclusive information that says Queen Nefertiti cannot have been alive up to and during the reign of

Tutankhamun.

Indeed, in order to be the age she appears to be in her last portrait, she would have had to be still there. In the aftermath of the Amarna period, Queen Nefertiti would certainly have been regarded as the wife of a reviled heretic, but there is no real reason to believe that her mummy would have been targeted for destruction beyond the usual rough handling of royal mummies by tomb robbers for the valuables their corpses contained.

Although the ultimate victor in the struggle for power that seems to have taken place in this part of the 18th Dynasty, Horemheb, razed Akhetaten, desecrated its royal tomb and is even thought to have exercised damnatio memoriae in the tomb of King Ay, his predecessor, we cannot be sure that he would have tried to completely obliterate her remains. Still, signs that there was animus directed against her by someone do exist.[51] Nevertheless, even though Thutmose III eventually destroyed the monuments of his ambitious aunt, Queen/King Hatshepsut, the other "woman-king" of the 18th Dynasty", I am convinced her mummy, in very good condition, is still with us. It makes sense that Nefertiti should have been removed from Amarna, where she was probably entombed, and be afforded a safe haven

---

51 Redford , **Akhenaten, the Heretic King** (page 228) "*The four major shrines were still standing, though somewhat dilapidated. The wreckers found as they approached that at Karnak, just as at Akhetaten (now largely abandoned), vandals had hammered out some of the reliefs here and there. The faces of the queen had often been hacked with hammer and chisel; less often had the king's visage been so treated.*"

in the tomb of a powerful ancestor of her husband's family, Amenhotep II, still in his sarcophagus and giving sanctuary to a number of displaced persons. Perhaps we ought to let go of our romantic notions about this royal lady, Nefertiti (The-beautiful-one-comes), take another look at the younger female from KV35 and concede that death is something against which even the greatest beauty rarely prevails.[52]

---

52 The text is the same as on the webpage, but I have broken up the sentences into more paragraphs for easier reading here. I have not changed the spellings of the names, even though I now use "Amun" in the theophoric names in this book in place of "Amen" and different writings of other names, as well.

Chapter Three

BLOOD AND TIME

Such were my thoughts and beliefs about Nefertiti and other matters in the year 1999. Today, I certainly don't stand by everything I wrote in that paper, and probably several of the scholars I have cited or quoted have changed their minds about some of their stances, as well.[53] I completely repudiate my theory that a small mummy [who has been genetically proved a male] could be Hatshepsut—although the idea of Gaston Maspero that this was Thutmose I probably has little more validity.

In a field like Egyptology, one always risks being wrong whenever one writes about anything. Yet everyone

---

53 For instance, Aidan Dodson no longer argues that the canopic coffinettes, found in KV62, originally belonged to Smenkhkare Djeserkheperu. He admits the cartouches were incised for a female ruler named Neferneferuaten, "effective for her husband".

realizes that the body of knowledge is always evolving and being in error is not fatal. People challenge one another, with their books and papers, to look closely at the topics, investigate further, even if that engenders contra viewpoints.

Retrospectively, I see that my own intuition about certain things in that paper has remained about the same as they are now. But my ideas about the Amarna Era and its aftermath are changing and evolving, too, if not radically. In 1999, I mentioned something about a coregency. This is how I view the subject today:

The controversy over the identification of the mummy of Queen Tiye has ended and one no longer needs to advocate it. However, I am still of the opinion that the age-at-death of Tiye is of the utmost importance to the question of a coregency between Amunhotep III, her husband, and Akhenaten, their son.

Some time after a mummy dubbed "the Elder Lady" was discovered in a side chamber of KV35, the tomb of King Amunhotep II, her identity and those of two other mummies lying on the ground beside her began to draw speculation. Some believed the Elder Lady, the Younger Lady, and the Young Prince [on account of his sidelock] must be the family members of Amunhotep II. Or perhaps the Elder Lady with her haughty features might even be Queen Hatshepsut! Although always deemed royalty, no one could conclude anything about these mummies because they were totally denuded, their shredded bandages lying around them. Nothing very obvious remained to serve as a clue to who they might be. All that was left was a single wig and that, too, was lying on the floor of the chamber.[54]

The day must have come when someone decided that the face of the Elder Lady resembled certain portraits of Queen Tiye, and so a hair sample was taken from the mummy to be microscopically compared with strands from a lock discovered in the tomb of the pharaoh Tutankhamun. The samples were a perfect match. The hair from the tomb was contained in a miniature anthropoid coffin inscribed with the name and titles of Queen Tiye.

As a result of the experiment with the hair, the Elder Lady became Queen Tiye for some, but many had their reservations. They argued that the mummy had not been old enough at the time of her death to be Tiye. In fact, the long, dark hair of this female was entirely without gray, according to the report of the anatomist, Dr. Grafton Elliot Smith.[55] He also noted, from his measurements, that this mummy was that of a delicate, diminutive lady, less than 5 feet in height. Smith opined her teeth were *"well worn but otherwise healthy"*. She had two ante-mortem ulcers on her left heel. There was nothing else to indicate to the naked eye what might have caused the death of the Elder Lady. Her upper torso has suffered very much at the hands of the tomb robbers.

It was concluded in a radiological study that x-rays of the skulls of the Elder Lady and Thuya, the mother of Queen Tiye, are similar enough to suggest that these

---

54 As it has a hanging braid as an element, it may be the wig of a sem-priest, an office held by Prince Thutmose, one-time heir of Amunhotep III, who was shown wearing this wig. Therefore, the Young Prince of the trio may be Thutmose.

55 G. Elliot Smith, MD, **The Royal Mummies** [1912] page 38.

mummies are related. As explained by Renate Germer,[56] the blood group of the Elder Lady indicated that she could have been a daughter of Yuya and Thuya at least theoretically. The blood group for both Yuya and Thuya is A2. However, Germer didn't know whether this meant A2A2 or A2O. In any event, if either Yuya or Thuya happened to have A2A2, then none of their children could have the blood type O, which is what the Elder Lady has. If both of the parents had A2O, then the chances of their children having A or O are 3:1 respectively.

Years later, the DNA study, done in Cairo,[57] confirmed the identity of the small mummy in question. She was, indeed, Queen Tiye and the electron microscopic hair test was vindicated as having told the truth of the matter. Although nothing was said about the Young Prince from KV35, the DNA showed that the Younger Lady was a daughter of Tiye and Amunhotep III. Not only that, she was the mother of King Tutankhamun. The father was her brother, whose remains ended up in KV55. This was a surprise that no one had expected, although there had been speculation upon the identity of the Younger Lady, as well. I proposed she was Queen Nefertiti sixteen years ago and I hold to my impression to this very day.[58]

56 Germer, Renate, "Die Angebliche Mumie Der Teje: Probleme Interdisziplinarer Arbeiten" SAK II: 85-90
57 "Ancestry and Pathology in King Tutankhamun's Family", JAMA, Zahi Hawass et al [2010]
58 Luban, Marianne, "Do We Have the Mummy of Nefertiti?", 1999, paper published online.

Wente and Harris, in their x-ray based study,[59] found the teeth of Queen Tiye to be better than Professor Smith had guessed them to be around 1912 and therefore assigned her an age range of 35-40, very problematic numbers to reconcile to the history of the great lady. Moreover, once she was finally removed from KV35 to join the other royals in the Cairo Egyptian Museum, bright lights required to film a documentary have revealed the henna dye in her hair. Therefore, it is not so certain that Tiye had no gray hairs although, when not illuminated, her long hair still lends the overall impression of youthful darkness. Smith described it as "brown, wavy, lustrous" and may not have noticed or cared to reveal the few nits amid the tresses, the remnant of the lice that the ancient Egyptians were forced to battle. Many have remarked on the beauty of the face of the queen, still striking despite all.

Because his father, Thutmose IV, died around the age of 30,[60] the next pharaoh, Amunhotep III, cannot have been very old when he was seated on the throne of Egypt. Just how young he was cannot be precisely known but a commemorative scarab, known as the Bull Hunt Scarab, gives the date Year 2 and mentions Queen Tiye. Even though the commemorative scarabs of Amunhotep III were made long after the events they describe, one is obligated to credit that the king had a queen by his

---

59 Wente, Edward F. & Harris, James E., **An X-ray Atlas of the Royal Mummies** (Chicago, 1980)
60 Professor Smith initially judged him to have been only 25, but later allowed the king can have been 28 or even older. His opinion regarding the KV55 remains was the same. Smith deemed the teeth of Thutmose IV "unworn".

second year of rule.[61] Under the circumstances, it is probably best to assume that Tiye, the daughter of Yuya, a relative of the king, and Thuya, his wife, was a child bride of no more than 9, selected due to her royal connections and already-evident beauty rather than her sexual maturity. In fact, her husband may not have been much older, himself, his bride perhaps chosen by his mother, the widowed Mutemwia.[62]

Since Amunhotep reigned for 38 years, it is reasonable to say that the surviving Great Royal Wife, Tiye, should have been about 45 years old. Without a coregency between her husband and her son, Amunhotep IV/Akhenaten, the dowager queen would have been around 60 years old if she died in Year 14 of her son, as has been thought.

In the preface of his "The Royal Mummies", Professor Smith made an important observation. He wrote: *"...with my present experience of the variability of the relative dates of epiphyseal unions in ancient Egyptian bones, I would make the reservation that the anatomical evidence, when based upon the penultimate stage of consolidation of a single bone, cannot be regarded as conclusive"* and *"...no bone is more misleading than the innominate bone; for I have found that the sulcus which separates the posterior part of the epiphysis cristae may remain open until middle age."*

What the professor of anatomy at the Cairo

---

61 Among those scarabs known to us, the only one lacking a date is the so-called "Marriage Scarab", which mentions the parents of Queen Tiye.

62 Who was not, however, actually attested as a queen during the reign of Thutmose IV.

School of Medicine meant is that the lack of complete fusion of the epiphyses does not necessarily mean an individual was 25 years old or less, despite what the text books stated. In the case of the KV55 individual, Smith noted that the leg bones were completely consolidated, meaning that the person must have been at least 24 years of age when he died.

And yet, at least one subsequent examiner of the KV55 bones, perhaps swayed by the unworn teeth and only recently erupted wisdom ones, was tempted to judge the deceased as having been as young as 18.[63]

While the hair of some persons remains relatively free from gray past middle age, it would seem odd that Tiye's teeth were viewed as only moderately worn by the dentist, Dr. James Harris, via x-ray—if she had lived to be as old as 60. The grit that got into the bread that even the royalty of ancient Egypt ate, due to the way the flour was ground, eroded the enamel of the teeth of an individual increasingly as time passed, causing very painful problems.

The teeth of the mummy of Amunhotep III are a nightmare. One wonders how he can have stood the pain from his abscesses. Amunhotep was a man of 50 or slightly more when he died, sick, grossly overweight, very short, bald, and lacking his front teeth. It may have been that the pharaoh had a greater liking for sweets made with honey than his wife. He may have not practiced oral hygiene, whereas Queen Tiye did, or she may not have

---

63 Impacted wisdom teeth seem to be a trait of the younger generations of the family. The KV55 individual and Tutankhamun exhibit the same.

had his predisposition for accumulation of tartar deposit. Smith found both the king's upper and lower teeth *"thickly encrusted with tartar"*. One can imagine how welcome the fat, middle-aged man was in the harem, although he had once been handsome enough.

The next assessment of the age of Tiye came from state-of-the-art technology, tomography or CT-scan. The conclusion was a wide range of 40-60 years old at death due to completed epiphyseal fusion and some degeneration of the spine and knees.[64]

The Younger Lady was estimated, by the same method, as having been 25 to 35 years old when she passed from life, despite unerupted wisdom teeth.

But for now it remains, all things considered, difficult to see the mummy of Queen Tiye as that of a woman of 60, regardless of having been blessed with better than average teeth. Her parents, Yuya and Thuya, were at least 60 when they died and their teeth evidence the usual problems of the elderly in ancient Egypt. Around 50 is probably a good compromise for the age-at-death of Tiye. It may be that Tiye's son, the man discovered in KV55, inherited his strong, resilient teeth from her.

Clearly, unless we can make a good argument for the two pharaohs, Amunhotep III and Akhenaten, having had a coregency, the more difficulties the mummy of Queen Tiye presents. Unfortunately, thus far unassailable proof of any coregency at all has been elusive. Cyril Aldred[65] took the stance that Amunhotep III and

64 According to the website of Dr. Zahi Hawass.
65 Aldred, Cyril, **Akhenaten, King of Egypt** (New York , 1988).

Akhenaten were coregents for as long as 12 years, a theory that may be the best possible one for allowing Queen Tiye to fit the age limitations that the remains, the Elder Lady, appear to mandate, even so Aldred obviously did not see Tiye as a mere child upon her marriage. I, myself, have problems with such a lengthy coregency. Yet it seems odd to me that Akhenaten would have celebrated a heb-sed so early in his reign, were it not a mirror heb-sed with that of his father, who celebrated his own jubilees in Years 30, 34, and 37. Therefore, it is difficult for me to envision that Akhenaten, as Amunhotep IV, can have been appointed coregent prior to Year 30. A coregency having begun as far back as Year 26 of Amenhotep III has very little evidence to support it.

If her son had already been a co-king as long as 12 years, it doesn't make a great deal of sense that Tushratta, the ruler of Mitanni, should have exhorted Akhenaten to ask his mother about the good relationship he had with Amunhotep III. Nor does it follow that Queen Tiye should have advised Tushratta to "*Promote your interests with Napkhururiya* [Neferkheperure], *watch him, and do not cease from sending pleasant delegations.*"[66] Should one believe that, for as long as 12 years, Akhenaten, already a full-grown man at the end of that period, had learned nothing about the affairs of state [despite, by his Year 4, already commissioning his own building projects at Karnak] and required "Mama" for an intermediary?

The letters that passed between the widowed Queen Tiye and King Tushratta strongly hint that a very young pharaoh was now on the throne by himself and

66 Redford, 1984.

nobody was certain of what his policies would prove to be, including his own mother! "Watch him" could very well mean "we must all wait and see what he will do with his unlimited power and that could be just about anything".

Moreover, other archaeological evidence perhaps renders such a lengthy coregency untenable. An official named Khaemhat[67] had a Theban tomb wherein he shows himself being given the gold of approbation by Amunhotep III in the latter's Year 30, the year in which the pharaoh celebrated the first of his three sed festivals.[68] No mention is made in this tomb of Akhenaten.

Another very important man named Ramose,[69] a vizier, also had a very large tomb prepared about the same time as that of Khaemhat; in fact, the reliefs in both tombs appear to have been carved by the same sculptor. Ramose, in his tomb portraits, has the "juvenilized" face of Amunhotep III [which the king used in his last years],but, for some reason, the pharaoh depicted in Ramose's tomb is Amenhotep IV.

Arthur Weigall, therefore, thought work ceased in the unfinished sepulcher of Ramose in the first few years of the reign of the man who later became Akhenaten. Weigall wrote: "*In an elaborate shrine sits the young King Amenhotep IV, represented with somewhat boyish features. Behind him sits the goddess Maat.*" But also "*...the names of Amun and Mut, and the word 'gods', have*

---

67 TT57, Khaemhat called Mahu.
68 Year 30, second month of the third season, day 27.
69 TT 55.

been cut out by the agents of the new religion of Aton,
who had instructions from Akhenaten to obliterate the
names of the old deities of Egypt. These have been
reinstated about the time of Seti Ist after the reversion to
the old religion of Amun."

If Weigall is correct in judging the tombs of the
two men to be from around the same time, [and I agree
they must be] then Akhenaten can have been made co-
king sometime during Year 34 of Amunhotep III as part
of the heb sed festivities but work on the tomb of
Ramose ceased before that, regardless, for unknown
reasons. Then, the tomb decoration was resumed after
the death of Amunhotep III. It is thought the brother of
Ramose, Amunhotep, steward of the king's residence at
Memphis and superintendent of the royal craftsmen, had
completed the work.

TT55, with its magnificently carved reliefs, must
have taken quite some time to decorate—longer than
tombs whose images are merely painted, so it was
certainly begun by Ramose while serving the only king
with whom he is closely associated, Amunhotep III. But
the tomb decoration included paintings to facilitate the
completion.

Another official, Si-mut, who was the Fourth
Prophet of Amun in Year 20 of Amunhotep III [and still
enjoyed this position in Year 34 during the second
jubilee, which was around the time he was elevated to
Second Prophet, according to Cyril Aldred], is shown in
the tomb of Ramose as being yet Fourth Prophet.

Aldred wrote that Si-mut was responsible for
building projects at Western Thebes during this period

and was probably the man in charge of preparing the tomb of Ramose for the vizier's burial. In a bid for some immortality of his own, Si-mut added his name to a portrait of himself on the south wall of the main hall and wrote the epithet "justified" for eternity, *"just as he did on a door-jamb at the temple of Amun in the Malkata palace. Thus, when he finished off the painting of the south wall* [of Ramose's tomb] *he had not yet reached the crown of his career, and the reign of Amunhotep III still had some years to run."*[70]

It is a mysterious situation and, therefore, nothing can be concluded with certainty about a coregency from this tomb.

Aldred mentioned some wine jar dockets from Amarna with Years 28 and 30 written on them. He opined these dates would have had to refer to a much longer reign than that of Akhenaten, who did not move to Akhetaten before Year 5 and, of course, died in his Year 17. So these dockets must certainly have come from the reign of Amunhotep III, the only king of the period who occupied the throne for so many years. The conclusion of British archaeologists, Pendlebury and Fairman, was that *"if the jars had reached Amarna full of wine and properly sealed, the contents must have been at least fourteen years old at the time of delivery; but as wine is presumed not to keep long in permeable pottery jars in a warm climate...it is most likely that Years 28 and 30 of Amenophis III were near to Year 6 of Akhenaten when Amarna began to be occupied by the official classes."*

---

70 Weigall, Arthur, **A Guide To the Antiquities of Egypt** (London , 1910).

While it is true that no wine jar dockets referring to the actual reign of Akhenaten were discovered in the city from prior to Year 6, I cannot uphold the idea of Pendlebury and Fairman that Year 6 corresponds to Year 30 but must speculate on the possibility of spoiled vintage. Even wine that is past its "expiration date" is surely still usable for an occasional libation offerings to the Aten.[71] It may also have happened that, when wine jars were reused, a scribe sometimes forgot to assign them a new date. I don't think we can allow twelve years of coregency, but four certainly seem possible.

As for Queen Tiye—if she was 9 years old in Year 2 of her husband, Amunhotep III, she would have been 41 in his Year 34 and 45 when he died. Year 38 [the last] of Amunhotep III can have been Year 4 of Akhenaten as Amunhotep IV. Ten years later, in Year 14 of the latter, Tiye can have died at age 55.

It is still not an ideal age-at-death given the appearance of her mummy. A coregency of 8 years seems far better. That is what the Spanish mission is advocating now on account of evidence they believe they have discovered in the tomb of Vizier Amunhotep, also called Huy, in the Asasif area.[72] The Spanish date the tomb to Year 30 of Amunhotep III. However, this interpretation of the evidence in the tomb, cartouches of both Nebmaare and Neferkheperure as co-rulers, is at odds with some

---

71 However, a wine label mentioning Year 31 was found in the tomb of Tutankhamun, also surely from the reign of Amunhotep III. Usually it was beer that was the beverage offered to the Aten.

72 Tomb No. 28. A team led by the Instituto de Estudios del Antiguo Egipto de Madrid and Dr Martin Valentin have been studying the tomb since 2009.

other things mentioned above.

It may be that the Bull Hunt scarab is incorrect in showing the cartouche of Queen Tiye beside that of Amenhotep III as early as his Year 2. No doubt it seemed, many years later, that the pair had been king and consort practically forever. Not everyone would have recalled precisely in what year of the kingship Tiye became the Great Royal Wife and it may not have mattered much in the long run. Even a young king, who has been instructed in the use of the bow, is capable of shooting bulls in an enclosure while he is protected from their horns. Since a king of Egypt was never expected to be monogamous, one had plenty of other diversion while waiting for the chosen queen to grow old enough to become a proper wife.

Isabella of Valois, second wife of Richard II of England, was probably even younger than Tiye. She was a little short of 7 years old when she became queen in 1396. But Canon Law decreed that the marriage could not be consummated until the bride was at least 12. In the case of Richard and Isabella, it never was, as the king went off on a crusade and died not long after. For all we know, Tiye was as young as Isabella of Valois when she became queen and that would shave a couple of more years off the age-at-death of her mummy.

At the time of the Year 30 heb-sed, Sitamun, who seems to have been the eldest daughter of Tiye and her husband, became a wife of her father. In those days, a girl of 12 or 13 was considered a woman and many were married at that age. Older was not considered "better". If Sitamun had been 13 in Year 30 of Amenhotep III, that means she was born in his Year 17. More likely, Sitamun was born long before. Perhaps she had been intended as a wife for her brother, Thutmose, who died, was considered too old for the new heir, Amunhotep, and there was no man of sufficient rank to marry her now except her own father. We do not know the reasons pharaohs took their own daughters as wives. The marriages may have been unconsummated. Perhaps such unions were recalled in the Bible when it stated that Pharaoh's daughter was childless and adopted Moses.

Due to high infant mortality, it is impossible to know how many children Tiye had borne by Year 30 and how many had died or been miscarried. Regardless of the truth about the age of Queen Tiye upon her death, this was once a lovely woman whose strong character is as plainly written on her face now as it surely was in life.

Head of Queen Tiye, discovered at Serabit el Khadim in 1905

Chapter Four

GENETICS

Obviously, having reached a new frontier in Egyptology, it is time for some long-cherished notions about the last years of the 18ᵗʰ Dynasty to be discarded. The DNA has spoken and, while it is clear that Amunhotep III married a relative, Tiye, [not someone out of the masses] unions between full brothers and sisters had not become passé with the demise of Dynasty 17.[73]

At the time of this writing, scholars and enthusiasts are having difficulty accepting the truth of this for several reasons. Several prominent Egyptologists have insisted, in writing, that the genetic picture can be interpreted as meaning that the parents of Tutankhamun could have been cousins instead of a full brother and sister. Apparently, they would rather trust in what what

---

73 Manetho, via Josephus, considered Thutmose I to be the first king of Dynasty 18 and he likely was.

the archaeological evidence *seems* to say than the DNA, which they do not quite know how to interpret. And they are not alone in clinging to the old theory that Akhenaten and Nefertiti must have been first cousins, the children of Queen Tiye and her brother, Ay, respectively. However, nowhere was it written in antiquity that Tiye had a brother named Ay. The only known brother is called Aanen, a man who was Second Prophet of Amun during the reign of Amunhotep III.

Ay, on the contrary, is not heard of, [had no known tomb in the Theban necropolis, as did Aanen[74]] until Akhenaten established his new city in Middle Egypt. How young can this so-called brother, Ay, have been if he had no status in the court of his brother-in-law, not being recognized as anyone important until the Amarna Era, some thirty years later?

While Ay may not have been the brother of Tiye and therefore not of any great consequence in her time as chief queen, he cannot have been exactly a nobody all along. Ay held the title of "it nTr" ["god's father"] and, given his importance to Akhenaten, he was perhaps a tutor to the latter while he was a prince—and even some sort of relative. In their deluxe tomb at Amarna, it is stated unquestionably that Ay's wife, Tey, had been a nurse of Nefertiti. Since the wet nurse of Tutankhamun, Maya, had been sufficiently valued to receive the royal boon of a very impressive tomb at Saqqara of the north, it must be considered that Ay's great status at Akhetaten can have been derived from his wife. There is nothing known at this time ruling out the possibility that Tey was

---

74 TT120.

the relative of Queen Tiye instead of Ay. Siblings bearing the same or very similar names was not something unheard of in ancient Egypt. Regardless, Tey and Ay must have been of the same generation as Tiye and Amunhotep III for Tey to have been a nurse of Nefertiti.

Ay had several grand titles, had doubtless become a wealthy man under Akhenaten, but there is nothing to indicate he had ever had a wife other than Tey.[75] If, as has previously been suggested, he had married his own daughter's nurse, that little girl must have been someone very special in order to become queen of Egypt. Yes, Nefertiti certainly was, but not in the way most Egyptologists, evidently, still believe.

Zahi Hawass and his team of experts sought the relatives of Tutankhamun. They assembled certain mummies, took samples of their DNA, and looked for genetic similarities, utilizing the same process for ascertaining the relationships of modern persons. The result is called "autosomal DNA". Our genetic profile has different names but it is all ultimately viewed as genes to which numbers are assigned. There is mitochondrial DNA, passed on in an unbroken chain from mother to daughter going back indefinitely. Males also receive mitochondrial DNA from their mothers, but they do not pass it on to their own offspring. Men pass on what is called yDNA to their sons, also in an unbroken line, but not to their daughters.

But there is autosomal DNA, which we all receive from both of our parents. Autosomal DNA is divided, on a chart, into loci. We get one allele at each microsatellite

75 The alliance of Ay and Ankhesenamun will be discussed anon.

or locus from each of our parents—that is, one combination of two—out of four possible combinations. That is because, at each marker or locus, our parents, themselves, have two alleles or genes, the ones they received from their own parents. At eight markers, the autosomal DNA of King Tutankhamun looks like this:

10/12	10/15	16/26	29/34
8/13	19/19	6/12	23/23

The fact that Tutankhamun has the same two numbers at both the 6th and 8th loci is indicative of his parents being related. But the king has **all** the numbers that the KV35YL and the male KV55 individual have at the same markers, in combinations. That means they are his mother and his father. By the same token, **both** of the parents of Tutankhamun have a combination of **all** of the same alleles or numbers that Amunhotep III and Queen Tiye have at their markers. It means they are both children of that couple and full siblings.

The oldest generation tested in Cairo consisted of Yuya and Thuya, who were not first cousins. Amunhotep III and Queen Tiye, of the next generation, may have been cousins, but they still do not have very much DNA in common at eight markers.

The DNA does not allow the parents of Tutankhamun to have been cousins. The autosomal DNA of even first cousins does not look like that of siblings. Full siblings share only about 50% of the same numbers at the loci [because each sibling has the potential to receive one out of four possible combinations of numbers from the same parents] and first cousins share even less—about 12.5%. Let's say one parent has 11/12 at one marker and the other parent has 10/16. A child could potentially inherit

10/11
10/12
11/16
12/16

but will only receive one set of numbers. Let's imagine one child gets 11/16 and the other child gets 10/12. Those are the only numbers each child can possibly pass down to his or her own children at that locus. Two unlikely cousins whose parents were **all** siblings [a brother and a sister being the parents of one cousin and another brother and a sister being the parents of the other] would still have different-appearing autosomal DNA from actual siblings. That is due to the recombining of the autosomal DNA numbers of the grandparents of the two cousins, whose four children did not receive the same numbers at all the loci.

Children of such incestuous unions would test out the same as full siblings **only** if **identical** twins reproduced with another set of identical twins, or if two identical twins reproduced with the same person. Identical twins have all the same DNA across the board. [If Amunhotep III reproduced with both Queen Tiye and her identical twin sister —a lady of whom we have never heard—which would still make any children the offspring of a king.] Twins who are not identical still have only about 50% of the same numbers at the loci, the same as other full siblings. You can see here that the KV35YL and the person found in KV55 share the normal amount for full siblings:

Younger Lady:

10/12	6/10	16/26	25/29
8/11	16/19	6/12	20/23

Male from KV55:

10/12	15/15	16/26	29/34
11/13	16/19	9/12	20/23

Moreover, there is nothing in the above graphs that prevents the KV35YL and the man from KV55 from having been non-identical twins![76] Yet there is no way that Ay and Tiye can have been identical twins or likewise Amunhotep III and a phantom sister in order to produce these two, if they are Akhenaten and Nefertiti, as cousins. At very most, all those mentioned can only have been fraternal twins, who, again, still share only

_____

76 Outside of the JAMA paper, an easy way to comprehend the royal relationships via the numbers is at:
http://ngm.nationalgeographic.com/2010/09/tut-dna/tut-family-tree

about 50% of their DNA like any other non-twin siblings.

Even if the KV35YL and the KV55 individual are not Nefertiti and Akhenaten, the odds of them being cousins or the offspring of two sets of identical twins are impossibly low. That Amunhotep III had identical twin-sister wives, Tiye and another woman, who bore these two, is more possible but not very probable. Ay simply does not fit into the equation at all.

On a Theban monument, Ay refers to Tutankhamun as his "son", this having been interpreted by some as meaning he was the king's grandfather. But the DNA indicates that Tutankhamun has 100% royal ancestry going back to Amunhotep III—at least. The boy's parents were a sibling prince and princess and there is nobody who can have been his grandfather **but** that very same Amunhotep III. Therefore, Ay must have used the term "son" in the same way that "it nTr" means a kind of father—neither denoting a near blood relative.

Nor can Nefertiti be ruled out as the mother of Tutankhamun because she is never styled "king's daughter"— and the KV35YL is certainly the daughter of Amunhotep III. She cannot be the daughter of some hypothetical twin brother of the pharaoh because she is also the child of Queen Tiye. During the reign of Akhenaten and for the remainder of the 18th Dynasty, no **queen** uses this title "king's daughter"—even though it is quite certain some of them, like Merytaten and Ankhesenamun, were the daughters of a king.[77]

---

77 Little Merytaten is styled "Hmt nswt sAt n Xt=f" at Karnak and likewise Neferneferuaten Jr. at Amarna, but both were too young to be queens. James Allen [2009] wrote of them "*If they are not simply*

Line drawing of Tey, nurse of Nefertiti, as seen in her
Amarna tomb, by M. Luban

The wait for the DNA has been a long one. There
were times when I despaired that the process, begun in
the '90's, would ever continue. Yet part of me always
hoped that it would resume, that someday the Egyptians
would permit another round of testing, knowing that our

*errors, they are perhaps to be read as 'daughter of the king's wife and
of his body.'"*

96

understanding of the 18th Dynasty could not go forward without it. Because of such optimism, I began to familiarize myself with the complexities of DNA. If I lived long enough to see any results, I wanted to be able to comprehend them.

In 1993-1994 Dr. Scott Woodward, then of Brigham Young University in Utah, was granted the right by the Egyptian authorities to take samples of DNA from the royal mummies of the New Kingdom. In 1996, an article about his work was published in the Sept/Oct issue of **Archaeology** magazine. The feature is titled "The Great DNA Hunt." Woodward stated that he expected only to be able to analyze mitochondrial DNA. Three years passed without any further publications or updates from Scott Woodward. In 1999, the scientist appeared in a Discovery Channel program. This documentary was called "Secrets of the Pharaohs." In it Woodward revealed that, over a span of eight generations of ancient Egyptian royalty of the 18th Dynasty, he had noted a "very narrow gene pool", that there had not been any marriages with anyone outside of the royal family.

A second version of this documentary was broadcast by PBS in 2001. By now Dr. Woodward had apparently formed some reservations. He had noticed a "minute variation" between a DNA sequence of Amunhotep I and his presumed successor, the first Thutmose. Therefore, intermarriage with a second family could have occurred.

Unfortunately, Scott Woodward, not being an Egyptologist, had to take the word of his Egyptian liaison, Dr. Nasri Iskander, when it came to who these mummies were. At that time, the Egyptians [and they were not alone] still believed that a small mummy from TT320 was that of Thutmose I. In a lecture,[78] the impressions of which were set down by Judy Greenfield in a publication named **Ostracon**, Woodward opined that Amunhotep I and Thutmose I were father and son. That they are father and son is probably true, but "Thutmose I", judging by the position of his arms, is a prince and not a pharaoh. The real mummy of Aakheperkare Thutmose I seems to have been lost. From what Woodward observed in their DNA, he perhaps meant that Amunhotep I sired the prince upon a woman who was not his own full sister. From our understanding of this part of Egyptian history, Amunhotep I had no surviving sons and the kingship passed to someone named Thutmose, whose father's name is not known from the archaeological record.

In the 2001 documentary, Dr. Woodward also stated that, while Dynasty 18 had begun with incestuous unions,[79] it had ended in the same manner. How he determined this I am not certain, as I don't think he was ever able to take a DNA sample from Tutankhamun, himself. Author Joyce Tyldesley seemed to be quite familiar with the DNA work of Scott Woodward and his

---

78 Presented on April 20, 2001.

79 He actually started his testing with what he believed was the final ruler of Dynasty 17, Seqenenre Tao, being advised that Ahmose I was the premier king of Dynasty 18. Strictly speaking, both Ahmose and Amunhotep I were also a part of the 17th Dnasty, However, the mitochondrial DNA of Ahmose and his son, Amunhotep I, were not the same, according to Woodward. Therefore, the mother of Amunhotep was not a full sister of King Ahmose.

BYU team and mentions it several times in her 2000 book, "The Private Lives of the Pharaohs". On page 143 she writes: "*While it has not been possible to extract a genetic profile for the smaller foetus, the larger baby has yielded a mitochondrial DNA sequence through which the scientists may be able to trace the maternal DNA of Ankhesenamen and her mother, Nefertiti.*"

Another source added that the microbiologist had obtained nuclear DNA from the foetus, as well. Nuclear DNA represents genetic information from both parents. Therefore, Woodward may have seen that the infant had some double numbers at certain loci [i.e homozygous alleles]—as did Tutankhamun, himself—and concluded her parents were closely related.

From my research, I have gathered that the royal mummies from which Scott Woodward was able to harvest some type of viable DNA probably were:

Seqenenre Tao
Ahmose I
Amunhotep I
"Thutmose I"
Amunhotep II
Thutmose IV
Yuya
Larger Foetus from KV62

Thutmose IV was not included in the later Cairo study, but Dr. Woodward **may** have noticed similarity between his DNA and that of Yuya. If so, that might have led Woodward to reason there was no marriage outside the royal family within this part of the dynasty.

That would not have made much sense at the time, knowing that Tiye was not a sister of Amunhotep III and **should** have introduced new mtDNA. But Dr. Woodward never indicated that he saw this so-called "new blood" —at least not according to any source that discussed his work. Actually, many of them, Yuya, Thuya, Amunhotep III, KV55 and Tutankhamun did have the same rare **blood type** of A2, according to Dr. Robert Connolly of Liverpool University. Queen Tiye had type O blood, but she is still the daughter of Yuya and Thuya. Connolly decided the larger foetus had type O, as well. Type O is not rare in Egypt.

One would have liked to discuss Dr. Woodward's work with him, get the correct facts from the main source, but he proved impossible to contact.

The later Cairo study publication in JAMA, already cited, confirmed some of the statements of Woodward. It showed that the parents of King Tut were a full brother and sister—and we can surmise from this that **at least** the mtDNA of Thuya, Queen Tiye, the Younger Lady, the KV55 individual, and Tutankhamun is identical. But that study does not indicate a full profile for the babies from KV62 or their putative mother—or any successful cloning of their mtDNA. Nor does it make known the mtDNA of Yuya or Amunhotep III.

It does indicate that the so-called wife of Tutankhamun [for the purposes of the study] was not his sister, but nothing evident there prevents her from having been a relative of the king.

Included in the Cairo DNA study was a mummy

referred to as KV21A—due to having been found by Giovanni Belzoni with another female mummy[80] in an undecorated tomb in 1817. The explorer, known as "The Italian Strongman", wrote:

"...This [tomb] is more extensive but entirely new and without a single painting in it. It had been searched by the ancients, as we perceived at the end of the first passage a brick wall, which stopped the entrance and had been forced through. After passing this brick wall you descend a staircase and proceed through another corridor, at the end of which is the entrance to a pretty large chamber with a single pillar at the center and not plastered in any part. At one corner of this chamber we found two mummies on the ground, quite naked, without cloth or case. They were females, and their hair pretty long and well preserved, although it was easily separated from the head by pulling it a little..."

A century and a half later, in 1989, archaeologist Donald Ryan entered KV21 again and, although the two mummies had been considerably damaged, he recognized that they had the raised left arms of queens and that their broken hands were clenched as though holding something. We know now that these royal ladies also suffered from talipes equinovarus to a marked degree. KV21A had two club feet [how she can have walked at all is difficult to know] and KV21B had one [the other foot is missing].

Even though she was severely crippled, the limited amount of autosomal DNA that could be harvested from KV21A convinced the Hawass team of scientists that this

---

80 Known as KV21B.

lady can have been the mother of the two still-born or miscarried female babies who were placed in the tomb of Tutankhamun, who seems to have been their father.

The photo of an anonymous mummified head [below] appears in another book of Dr. G. Elliot Smith, "Egyptian Mummies" [1924]. The remains has a long neck and the long hair described by Belzoni. KV21A is missing her head. Can this be it? One is reminded of the flowing locks of Queen Tiye. Although 18th Dynasty ladies are portrayed wearing wigs, the evidence shows they sometimes grew their natural hair down to their shoulders, at least.

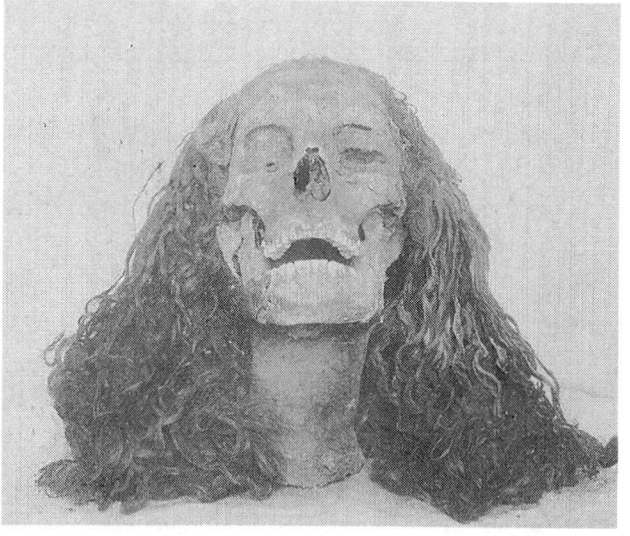

A reason that KV21A cannot be a daughter of the KV55 individual is because, at the first locus, she has been given the numbers 10/16, whereas the parents of Tutankhamun both have 10/12 at that marker. Remember that a person cannot have a number that two others do not possess to donate—and still be their child. At the 6th locus KV21A has yet another number that the mother and father of Tutankhamun do not possess there.

One of the most interesting aspects of this mummy's DNA profile is that she has the allele 35 at the marker D21S11, not seen there since the profile of Thuya. Allele 35 is rather rare at the locus, but makes the biggest showing in Africa, not so much Egypt where it is shown at 0.0110. Elsewhere in Africa it is definitely higher at the locus. Otherwise, in the Middle East, there is only Turkey, the So. Adana Area having the highest at 0.0070.[81] These numbers come from the DNA of modern populations, but this may be indicative of the distant past, as well.

Also, KV21A has an extremely rare allele, 16, at the first locus, which she shares with Amunhotep III. In fact, her numbers at the locus are 10/16, exactly the same as the king. Since 16 is a much rarer allele at the first locus than 35 is at the fourth, this is most interesting. What's even more interesting is that allele 16 at the first marker is most common in Hispanic lands and those settled or invaded by Hispanics—like Oman, to which came the Portuguese. Otherwise, 16 at the locus seems pretty much null in the Middle East.

---

81 Adana is a large city, 19 miles inland from the Mediterranean Sea, in south-central Anatolia. Some believe that the name is a Hittite one and also pertains to the Denyen, one of the Sea Peoples who were a threat to Egypt. Others have theorized that Adana refers to Danaeus, an Egyptian who left his native land on account of a feud with his brother, Aegyptus. It does seem possible that 35 at the locus was brought to Anatolia from Egypt.

Neither of those numbers are present at the first locus in Yuya, Thuya, or their daughter Tiye.[82] As for the 10 of KV21A at the 6th locus, nobody has it there in the entire family tree until KV21A and the next generation. So it is difficult to say just how KV21A is related to the other persons who were subjects of the Cairo study. But further test results from these mummies, utilizing the "next generation sequencing" process, might help answer the questions.

Also interesting is that Foetus 1 at D7S820 has the number 13, not seen in the generations at that locus since Thuya.

It would have been edifying to include Thutmose IV, the father of Amunhotep III, in this family tree. Since the parents of Queen Tiye were tested, another generation from the patrilineal side would have aided in showing what "royal DNA" of the 18th Dynasty looks like. Or, rather, which alleles Amunhotep III got from his father. That way we might get a better idea of how someone like the ladies KV21A and B, the foetus—or Yuya— were related to the royal line.

There can be little question, however, that Yuya was a relative of Amunhotep III. They share alleles at five of the eight markers, too many for it to be coincidental. This goes a long way toward explaining why the young pharaoh was married to Tiye, Yuya's daughter. But, again, without the DNA profile of Thutmose IV, we cannot tell

82 This allele 16 at the locus is hardly to be found anywhere. Nor is it even especially common in the Iberian Peninsula. It makes some showing in Spain and among the Basques and a bit in Brazil and Venezuela, doubtless from Spanish influence.

if Yuya was related to Amunhotep's mother or his father. My guess is—and this is mere speculation—the allele 10 that Amunhotep III introduces into the presently-known family tree at the marker D13S317 is non-Egyptian and may have been contributed to the gene pool via a foreign female. 10 at this locus does not make a very good showing in north Africa [Egypt, pooled, has only .0631 and central Egypt, el-Minia, does slightly better with .0830] or in Africa in general. However, the farther east of Egypt the higher the frequency, from Anatolia to India and best of all, the Far East. In other words, it is an Asiatic allele, with ratios as low in Europe as in most of Africa.[83]

So we do not know precisely who this so-called wife of Tut and the mother of the mummified babies can have been, but she is not not, in my opinion, the Ankhesenamun who was the daughter of Akhenaten and Nefertiti. Nor, in the absence of many alleles, is it even certain that KV21A really was the mother of either foetus from KV62. One would find it very odd that a girl so deformed would have been given to a king of Egypt for his chief wife or even a concubine.

The 18th Dynasty royals are an enigmatic group. Not only is the blood group of many of them, A2, very rare in modern Egyptians, but their autosomal alleles are sub-Saharan, Iberian, and Asiatic, some of them belonging to only 1 in a 1,000 modern persons. One longs to know how it came to be.

A big concern in the Egyptological community is

_____

83 Since it was written that Thutmose IV was able to acquire a bride from the king of Mitanni, that may have been Mutemwia.

"contamination", meaning people are worried that the DNA of the royal mummies might belong to one of the modern individuals who have handled them over many years. Such doubting takes very little of both the method of extraction of the DNA and the precautions of the laboratory process into consideration. The DNA was not harvested from parts of the body that can have been contaminated but from inside bone.

Besides, the mummies, themselves, provide their own checks and balances. Some were securely identified prior to the DNA testing and so other mummies suspected of being near relatives must match to their recombined autosomal DNA. The genes of an outsider would raise an instant red flag. Even if, say, Howard Carter or Victor Loret had, by some miracle, been descendants of the 18th Dynasty, that would not be reflected in their autosomal DNA—at all—they being so far removed from the royal mummies in time. The only way Howard Carter's DNA can be mistaken for a son of someone like KV55 is via yDNA—providing Howard Carter was a long-lost British scion of the 18th Dynasty and never had the slightest clue. However, once again, the test results of the Cairo project show autosomal DNA—which is not yDNA. Testing for the latter would not be able to include any female mummies.

The same applies to an Egyptian like Zahi Hawass or Dr. Yehia Gad, a molecular geneticist, who worked on the project. Seeking the autosomal DNA of the mummies, their own would never be confused with that of a near relative of the royals.

After the publication of this team of scientists in

106

JAMA, there was quite a negative reaction from some people in the field of microbiology. The nay-sayers simply could not believe that ancient DNA could be successfully cloned, probably because they had not done it, themselves. It is now easier to understand why Scott Woodward never published his own work with the royal mummies in a scientific journal. But, since 2010, DNA from Egyptian animal mummies has been sequenced and identified as belonging to their correct species—and the critics have fallen silent.

Chapter Five

THE ROYAL COUPLE

Another myth that can be disproved is that the gorgeous Nefertiti was forced to marry a man who was perhaps the ugliest pharaoh of Egypt ever to rule the land. The beauty of the queen was praised in writing even by her husband, so there is no reason to believe her likenesses existed to flatter her. However, that Nefertiti had no choice but to become the wife of Akhenaten is probably the truth.

The shared genes of siblings create a potential for them to look quite a bit alike, even if one is a male and the other a female. On his earliest kingly statues, the young Amunhotep IV is portrayed as appearing quite normal and even boyishly handsome. The similarity of his face to that of Nefertiti is striking. The main difference is the pharaoh's elongated chin, which saves him from looking effeminate. Like Nefertiti, he has a very long neck—which would continue to be a feature of

108

his portraits even in that future period at Akhetaten when he began to be shown in a manner that has been rightfully called "bizarre".

Because they were brother and sister, Akhenaten and Nefertiti touted themselves as the living incarnations of the deities, Shu and Tefnut, twins that sprang from the sun-god, Re. These children of Re were also husband and wife in the mythology. Whether they were actual twins or not, for Nefertiti to be the only [official] goddess at Akhetaten until Year 9 of her husband's reign, on the same par with Akhenaten as a product of the sun, would have seemed strange if she was a known commoner or even a foreigner. In the tomb of Ay and Tey at Amarna, the queen is referred to as "the goddess" [nTrt].

My theory is that the odd and even grotesque artistic styles seen in the royal portraits from Tell el Amarna came about as the result of Akhenaten realizing he resembled Nefertiti and resenting the fact. What man, especially one who wishes to be viewed as a powerful ruler, wants to look like his swan-necked wife? Certainly, Akhenaten was not the beauty that Nefertiti was, but there was something rather droll in their circumstances. A cute matched set in age and appearance, both waiting in the wings as children to become king and consort.

The gods might marry one another in a mythological sense but, in reality, a match between a brother and a sister can hardly be viewed as ideal by the parties, propaganda aside. They may have loved one another in a way, but at least Akhenaten had the

109

consolation of knowing he would never be stuck with Nefertiti as his sole sexual partner. The queen had no such solace, unless she wished to risk being a traitor to the crown. One hopes that Nefertiti, in time and as Akhenaten grew older and matured, was able to see him more in the light of a husband instead of her brother. Exactly what this pair privately thought of one another we will never know.

It is quite likely that the visage of Akhenaten did change somewhat in the way that most men's faces have of becoming more coarse than when they were boys. In fact, some males hardly retain the same features they possessed before the onset of puberty. They either become more handsome in a masculine way or far less attractive than when they were pretty lads. But Akhenaten, in my opinion, was not yet an adult when he became a king. I feel certain it was he, once he managed to get control over his own image, who instructed his craftsmen to make him look as different from Nefertiti as possible and to exaggerate his features in any way they chose in order to accomplish that.

Surely it was not a choice of the artists and sculptors, as such capricious license would have amounted to treason. also. It is difficult to credit that any royal portrait maker in the history of the world has ever striven to render his sovereign uglier in his art than he was in real life. Men may be vain or not, but kings are routinely flattered by those who hope to retain their commissions or even their heads. Even if he is truly homely, a monarch can be made to look dignified, even majestic, by a skilled artist. Except perhaps in the case of the Hapsburg rulers of Spain, the worst-looking collection of crowned heads ever.

At Akhetaten, the pharaoh appeared just plain outlandish. Not only was he not handsome, usually, but the only thing majestic about him is the crown on his own head. The chin is long, the lips are coarse and boorish in their thickness. The eyes are slanted, at their worst in a sinister fashion. The nose is long and sloping, hardly noble. One can see that the sweetness of the early portraits has entirely vanished.

A big belly hangs over the king's kilt. He looks like a man who is too fond of food or beer or both. The arms are thin, by contrast, and the shoulders narrow—a far cry from the athletic way in which the previous 18th Dynasty rulers were shown with their slim waists and broad shoulders. Akhenaten was surely short, but sometimes he was made to appear taller—well, he was always portrayed as taller than anyone else, sometimes by a great deal. The KV55 skeleton is under 5' 4", according to Professor Smith, or less than 1m 651mm. The KV35YL measures at 5'2"—so these two were approximately the same height.

However, King Akhenaten did not manage to look different from Nefertiti for long. This was because it was the artistic custom for the ruler's family members to be shown with his features, especially when they were portrayed with him or near him. It was also normal for the officials of the crown to have the pharaoh's face on their portraits and funerary equipment instead of their own—although it didn't seem to happen at Akhetaten. This sort of deference was thought the king's due, as he

111

owned everything and everybody in Egypt in a general way. Statues and tombs were only possible as a result of the sovereign's favor and generosity. There were no freelance artisans who could be hired for a price. All worked for the pharaoh, although they could labor on their own tombs, if they could find the time. Or they could help out with each other's tombs if they lived in a place like the craftsmen's village at Deir el Medina. But it was written that no one could have a tomb at all without the permission of the pharaoh.

One of the least repulsive reliefs of Akhenaten from Tell el Amarna

Queen Nefertiti stripped of beauty in the worst innovative style[84]

Before very long Nefertiti began to appear as ugly as Akhenaten, at least on the reliefs. Obviously, her statues continued to demonstrate her beauty. It was not exactly an unprecedented phenomenon in ancient Egypt—that a queen should look less than attractive at all times—because Tiye, also, was not always shown as pretty. We know for certain now that the mummy, the Elder Lady, is Tiye and the face of the corpse retains beauty even in death. Queen Tiye must have been good-looking and yet all her likenesses don't lend this impression. Since she wasn't the sister of Amunhotep III and probably looked nothing like him [except that they both were very short, even for ancient Egyptians], it is difficult to know the reason Tiye was not considered a beauty by the sculptors of her day, someone to celebrate in the art. Perhaps it was because her eyes were small

---

84 Brooklyn Museum, sandstone fragment.

and her chin too recessive. The lips of Queen Tiye can only be described as "luscious" and her nose was fine. The features of Amunhotep III look not unattractive in most of his portraits, although not exactly noble.

Amunhotep III, limestone, Berlin Museum

The king, like his spouse, had full lips and a receding chin. Viewed in profile, his nose was of the snub variety, which Akhenaten certainly did not inherit—although Tutankhamun did. Some of his statues make him appear to have had the shape of a short pregnant woman. Thus appeared the most influential and wealthiest man in the known world, standing no taller than five feet in height.

Ever since Dr. Hawass et al published the JAMA paper on the DNA of the family of Tutankhamun, there has been, among the online Egyptophiles, the knee-jerk reaction that, because she has now been confirmed as a daughter of Amunhotep III and Queen Tiye, the mummy, the Younger Lady from KV35, cannot possibly be Queen Nefertiti. But the fact remains I first got the idea that KV35YL could be Akhenaten's wife because of physical resemblances of the mummy to the portraits of the queen. There are quite a few, and I pointed them all out in my paper, previously shown here. I do admit to having had doubts that the KV35YL can have been a daughter of Amunhotep III and Queen Tiye because their [at the time purported but now confirmed] mummies are excessively short in stature and the KV35YL is taller. At 5' 2", the YL is taller than her father and certainly taller than the 4' 9" Queen Tiye. The YL is of an average height for a woman of ancient Egypt. However, each successive generation seems to have grown to be a little higher, ending with a 5' 6" Tutankhamun, the average size of an ancient Egyptian male.

No matter what arguments people line up against the KV55 individual and the KV35YL being Akhenaten and Nefertiti, it seems an undisputed fact that Amunhotep III and Queen Tiye had a daughter who looked like Nefertiti, possessed the physical attributes evidenced by that lady's portraits [when she was allowed to look like herself and not like a strange version of

115

Akhenaten]. Put differently, Amunhotep III and Queen Tiye were capable of engendering a Nefertiti or someone who resembled her greatly—down to the extraordinarily long neck. Logic and DNA dictate it must be so. After I had proposed that the KV35YL might be Nefertiti, another woman, Susan James, took a good look at the Elder Lady and concluded that *she* looked like Nefertiti and advocated this identification. There is no hope for Ms. James' theory now, but perhaps James' perception of similarity was not far off the mark. The resemblance was that between a mother and a daughter, nothing unexpected at all.

Akhenaten is depicted as being very affectionate with Nefertiti and their daughters, as well. We have already seen the king holding his mother by the hand. Such artistic displays of intimacy by a pharaoh with his family members was unprecedented. But Akhenaten kisses his wife and children and allows even the queen to sit on his lap, her bare feet dangling.

It may have happened that, prior to their early marriage, Akhenaten had never seen very much of Nefertiti. Amunhotep III, hardly monogamous, appears to have had many daughters and possibly numerous sons, too—although the only ones who counted in the succession were the princes born of the Great Royal Wife, Tiye. So the boys and their governors and tutors may have lived separately from the girls and their attendants in the harem. In fact, there is evidence that the princes were given to certain trusted friends of the pharaoh to be raised in their private homes—truly in the manner of actual "godfathers". Perhaps these "tutors" were instructed not to spoil the lads so that they had a chance to grow up as normal men—until they finally became gods. If this was the case, then familiarity did not necessarily remind one every day that one had married a sister. It was even possible to fall in love if one viewed the sibling as little more than a stranger in the beginning and no one had suggested there was anything untoward in the coupling.

However, if Tey was a nurse of Nefertiti [and Egyptian infants fed at the breast for a long time] and her husband, Ay, was really a tutor of Akhenaten, then perhaps the two children had been raised together. Also, for Tey to have had the milk to nurse Nefertiti, there would have had to have been a child of Tey of around the same age. Regardless, there was a northern vizier named Aperel [tomb found by Alain Zivie at the Bubasteion] who was also styled "it nTr". How was he involved in the tutoring or mentoring of the future ruler? This title of "god's father" is so uncertain of meaning that one suspects it can have been purely honorary.

Since Nefertiti was exquisite and Akhenaten was at the point where boys usually become obsessed with their sexuality when their union was arranged, there may not have been a single obstacle that prevented Nefertiti from becoming a part of that obsession.

At Akhetaten, Princess Merytaten is eventually depicted with breasts and with her head covered by a wig like an adult. This is in contrast to her younger sisters, who still have a shaved skull with the exception of a decorated lock of hair. This indicates that Merytaten had already achieved or was entering puberty. Certainly, she would have been a grown woman at the end of her father's reign. At about the same time that Akhenaten was crowned, Merytaten was born. Even at Karnak, prior to the move to Akhetaten, she is already seen as a small figure standing behind her mother, Nefertiti.

It may seem very strange to us that a lad of 13 or 14 should be a father, but for all the centuries up to perhaps the second half of the 19th of the modern era, it was not thought remarkable. The Jews, an oriental people who, nevertheless, lived in the West, due to having been displaced by the Romans, often married their children off at a very young age. For example, Solomon Maimon, an intellectual and philosopher, who was born in 1753 in what is now Belarus in Eastern Europe, was married at the age of 11. By the time he was 14, he tells us in a memoir, Solomon was already a father. Such married couples, of course, did not live on their own but with the parents of one of them, preferably the more well-off. In those times, young Jewish men who were scholars were not expected to earn a living and could devote their time to their studies.

The youthful Amunhotep IV certainly had no worldly cares and, since he was a coregent with his father when he became a king, probably did not concern himself with the affairs of state, either. Within a few years, he had formed some strong opinions about religion. The future Akhenaten, at the time of his move to his newly constructed city, was precisely at the age when one becomes idealistic, which is to say 17 or 18 years old. As my grandson and his cousin, the son of my sister, demonstrated extreme intelligence at that age, I have no difficulty envisioning a young man, hardly more than a boy, having the knowledge and capability of many much older men.

Professor G. Elliot Smith had quite a lot to say, in writing, about his study of the KV55 remains. Because he was not an Egyptologist, he had to take his cue from others when it came to the history of Akhenaten—all being then in agreement that the bones were of that ruler. In "The Royal Mummies", Smith needed to prove that, while the individual was young, he was not too young to "...*satisfy the demands of the historians as to Khouniatonou's age.*" The anatomist also wrote: "*There is information suggesting he was a minor at the time of his father's death and that he reigned for seventeen years. Surely, then, there need be no great straining of the evidence to bring the anatomical and historical facts into harmony, the one with the other.*"

With these sentiments I wholly agree. Even if the KV55 mummy had been given the coffin of another king, that being Akhenaten, what can have been the reason so-called "magic bricks", two of them bearing the name of the heretic, would be placed around it? An ancient Egyptian brick was not difficult to make. One put mud into a mold, the mud being reinforced by other materials like chopped straw. Before the brick had completely dried and hardened in the sun, one could stamp it with a seal or write on it with a sharpened stick. If it was not Akhenaten in that coffin, the new occupant can have been supplied with his own bricks easily enough.

Chapter Six

CHRONOLOGY

In my book, "Manetho Demystified",[85] I proposed the possibility that the Egyptian historian assigned 12 years of rule to all the kings he associated with the ruined city of Akhetaten because no tomb there gives a higher date than Year 12. Regardless of being omitted from subsequent kinglists due to being tainted by the heresy of Neferkheperure Akhenaten, these pharaohs called "Acencheres" by Manetho must still have somehow been remembered up to the Ptolemaic era. That "Acencheres" can be a writing of Ankhkheperure nobody disputes.[86]

According to Manetho, the first "Acencheres" was a woman, the daughter of a king.[87] He may have been

---

85 Pacific Moon Publications, 2012.
86 That is Manetho per Josephus. Africanus renders it "Acherres", instead, has only two kings by that name and says nothing about either being a female.
87 If the Younger Lady from KV35, the mother of Tutankhamun, is

correct on both counts, but an element from a box, discovered in KV62, the tomb of Tutankhamun, indicates that the first Ankhkheperure must also have been called Neferneferuaten—namely Nefertiti. This last is also shown in a smiting pose, usually reserved for kings in the art. She is, moreover, portrayed on a stela, wearing a kingly crown, with her husband, who caresses her under the chin. Due to the elevation of the status of the "great royal wife", that vacant title is now assumed by the eldest daughter of the couple, Merytaten. Precisely why Akhenaten decided to make Nefertiti his coregent at some point cannot be known, but it was clearly intended to be a temporary arrangement. For one thing, Akhenaten had children who had precedence over everyone in the order of succession. Secondly, the cartouches of Ankhe[t]kheperure Neferneferuaten contained the words "beloved of Waenre" and "beloved of Neferkheperure", the prenomina of Akhenaten, which would not be proper except in the case of a coregent pro tem. In the cartouches of sovereigns, they are beloved only of the gods.

In 1988, James Allen separated Neferneferuaten from another pharaoh, who also used the prenomen of Ankhkheperure. This was a male ruler, Smenkhkare Djeserkheperu. Although at one time these two persons were considered one and the same, they are clearly not. The cartouches of Smenkhkare do not include that he was beloved of Akhenaten and therefore his rule was not considered—at least by himself—to be a conditional one,

---

Nefertiti, then her DNA indicates she was the daughter of Amenhotep III and Queen Tiye.

based on association.

Inscription of box element, after H. Carter

One can see, above the cartouche of Merytaten in the right-hand column, that she has the title of "queen" but is not styled "king's daughter"—and this inscription would have been made in the reign of her father, whose cartouches are on the extreme left. Merytaten is never called "king's daughter" above any surviving cartouche from her queenship.

Even though in the Hellenistic era of the Ptolemies there was perhaps a little more remaining for viewing of the kingship of Neferkheperure Akhenaten besides at what is now called Tell el Amarna,[88] the historian, Manetho, did not include him in his kinglist in a recognizable manner. There does not appear to be anyone with a name like Neferkheperure, at least. The historian, who wrote in the Greek language, does seem to have been aware of the successors of a king he called "Oros", writing their names as "Acencheres". None of the

Akhenaten and his female coregent

persons called "Acencheres" are assigned a duration longer than 12 years by Manetho, as has been mentioned.

88 For example, an Aten temple at Heliopolis, its blocks being used, after the Arab conquest, for the construction of a mosque.

This is probably because the latter had seen, read, or heard that there was a ruined city in Middle Egypt in which had lived an unusual king and that no inscription there was dated beyond Year 12 + x months.

Although two tombs at Tell el Amarna, those of Huya and Meryre II, do show a triumphal scene, often dubbed the Great Durbar, bearing the datum Year 12 II prt 8, there seems to have been no more work done on any of the tombs of the officials except that of Meryre II. Adjacent to the durbar tableau in his tomb, there appears a new pharaoh named Ankhkheperure Smenkhkare, accompanied by his queen, Merytaten, who is surely the eldest daughter of Akhenaten and Nefertiti. However, the scene with the new king and his consort was left unfinished.

Akhenaten is assigned a reign of 17 years due to an inscription on two wine jars, that have Year 17 overwritten by Year 1. After Year 6, there are wine jar dockets found at El Amarna representing every regnal year to 17. A recently published inscription with a Year 16[89] of Akhenaten mentions Queen Nefertiti, indicating she was still alive at the time and had been superceded as Great Royal Wife by no other woman. But she is Ankhkheperure Neferneferuaten no longer.

The following are some points regarding the co-regency problem: If king Akhenaten had a spouse whom he trusted to elevate to the status of coregent, why would he have wanted or needed a male coregent as early as Year 12—it having been taken for granted that the

89 Year 16 III Akhet day 15, found in a limestone quarry at Deir Abu Hinnis.

124

appearance of Smenkhkare as king around the corner from the Great Durbar scene indicated his appointment in that very year or soon after? Alternatively, to believe that Smenkhkare had been appointed late in the reign of Akhenaten makes no more sense, as by then the older pharaoh had a son and a daughter who was already a grown woman by Egyptian standards. Since Nefertiti was still alive and Merytaten of age, both being suitable regents for the child, Tutankhaten, the introduction of a male co-king cannot be fathomed—even if he was already the husband of Merytaten.

Nor can Smenkhkare have been an older son of Neferkheperure Akhenaten—and still be the body placed in KV55. Since there are only two candidates for the identification of the remains of a man discovered in that makeshift tomb, those being Akhenaten and Smenkhkare, DNA testing has shown this king must be a son of Amunhotep III and Queen Tiye. Since the Hermopolis block states that Tutankhaten was the son of a king and the KV55 individual is his father, Tutankhaten's grandfather must be Amunhotep III—and not Akhenaten.

In my opinion, Akhenaten was still a very young man in his Year 12. He is depicted as king [Amunhotep IV] on a lintel over the entrance to the Theban tomb of Kheruef,[90] accompanied by his mother, Queen Tiye, and not a wife. Whether he was made a coregent with Amunhotep III or merely succeeded him and portrayed on the lintel on account of that, the new

---

90 TT 192. The tomb scenes indicate that Amunhotep III had at least 16 daughters.

pharaoh need have been no older than 13 at the time and can have been as young as 30 when his reign was over. In the intervening years, there was plenty of time to sire

The future Akhenaten with his mother, Queen Tiye

seven children, including an heir, Tutankhaten.

Clearly, Akhenaten was not the eldest son of Amunhotep III and no one can know when he was born. The one-time heir apparent was another prince, called Thutmose after the father of Amunhotep III, who seems to have died at a young age. No one can know when Smenkhkare was born, either, but those who believe the KV55 remains are his, have concluded this due to the

126

young age at death assigned to the mummified corpse, now only a skull and bones. Those who examined the KV55 individual [before the CT-scan] had their slightly varying opinions. It can only be an estimate as there is no such thing as precise—in this case perhaps a window of 18–25 years, making allowances for the examination of the bones without technology. For instance, Douglas Derry concluded an age of about 23 and Eugen Strouhal gave an age range of 19 to 22.

There can hardly be any doubt that Tutankhaten, meaning "the living image of the Aten", was the ideal name for the heir of an Atenist king. Because the name is so perfect for a future Atenist ruler, it rather testifies against Akhenaten having had any sons, living or dead, who were older than Tutankhaten. The father, having relinquished the name of Amunhotep, chose for himself one that meant "beneficial to the Aten". Akhenaten had once worshipped the old Egyptian gods, as everyone knew, but his son and heir apparent would be the first pharaoh ever born who could say he knew no other religion except that devoted to the sun. He was pure because his lips had never uttered a prayer to another deity. Therefore, it was appropriate to call him the living image of his sole god, the Aten.

That the youth who later became Tutankhamun died at a young age is a given, but his exact age at death cannot be known because it is not possible to pinpoint this from human remains except within a range of a few years. Tutankhamun could have been anywhere from 18 to 21 when he passed from life. It is thought that he ruled for 10 years maximum,[91] which made him from 8 to 11 years old at his accession. That would indicate that his father could have been a minimum of 14 years old when he was born.[92] At the lower end of the estimate for the age at death of Tutankhamun, which is 18, and if he became king in his 8th year of life, his predecessor/father ought to have been at least 22 when he died.

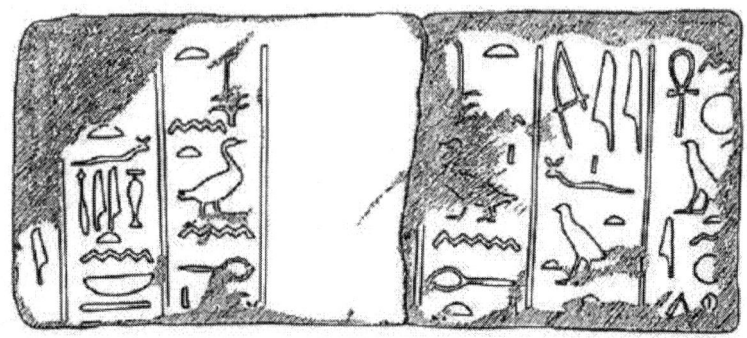

Blocks found at Hermopolis mentioning "king's son" Tutankhaten and a princess.

If Tutankhamun was 11 when he was crowned, it mandates that his father was at least 25 when he vacated the throne. This is the math pertaining to the possibility of Smenkhkare having sired Tutankhamun but it is only applicable if the father was so very young, only 14, when the son was born. It also depends on the estimates of Derry and Strouhal being correct when it comes to the age at death of the KV55 individual.

If the estimates were too low and the few extra

---

91 Last year on wine jar labels from his tomb.
92 Mother possibly impregnated when the father was 13.

years needed for a young age at death for Akhenaten are possible, then the situation is much different.

Akhenaten, even though he probably began his own procreative history just after puberty, evidently had nothing but daughters up to Year 12 of his kingship. But that pharaoh had 5 remaining years during which to get a son—and no more. This would indicate that, Akhenaten being his father, Tutankhamun can have been a maximum of 5 years old when Akhenaten died. In that event, someone else needed to have reigned in the interim between the ages of 5 and 8 of Tutankhamun for 3 years and possibly more if he was somewhat older at his accession.

As has already been pointed out, the fact that a new king, Smenkhkare, is depicted around the corner from an important scene in the tomb of Meryre II[93] has prompted some persons to conclude that Smenkhkare was chosen as a coregent by Akhenaten soon after the Year 12 festivities. But was he really chosen at any point? Was he simply a man, even a relative of Akhenaten, who decided to take advantage of the fact that the true heir was a mere helpless child, shades of the situation much earlier within the 18th Dynasty, when a king's widow, Hatshepsut, had managed to push aside a boy and overshadow him for numerous years?

Queen Tiye appears to have died before her son. Her age at death has been discussed earlier in this book. Nefertiti, herself, very likely outlived Akhenaten and was

---

93 One of the "northern tombs" of the city. Meryre II, in addition to being in charge of the palace of Nefertiti, was "Overseer of the Two Treasuries".

about 30 years old. Merytaten became the wife of the new king—and possibly Ankhesenpaaten, the next eldest living sister, as well. They were very young women in their mid-teens. This particular usurper would not have cared if the older girl had been a wife of her own father, nominally or in reality.

That Smenkhkare was already the husband of Merytaten at the time of his kingship is not so likely, although possible. The eldest princess had been given the title of "Hmt nswt wrt" previously, which means "Great Royal Wife" and that means the wife of Akhenaten, himself—not his coregent, who was a woman. When Nefertiti no longer served in that capacity, was Merytaten demoted? Not likely, and therefore Akhenaten had two queens, one called "Hmt nsw wrt" and the older "Hmt nsw aAt".[94] Without the first, the second title would not have been needed as a distinction between two women. Also, there had been another wife, Kiya, and she had been referred to as "Hmt mrrty aAt", yet another distinction. Egyptian pharaohs sometimes married their own daughters, but there is no evidence that they later gave them over to other men.

But one thing is certain; Smenkhkare, whom we shall call a counter-king, was an Atenist or at least a devoté of the cult of Re. He could have lived anywhere in Egypt, but apparently the new city of Akhetaten, with its sun temples and beautifully-decorated palaces, suited him well enough to add to its construction. Nothing changed in the land where the official religion was

_____

94 But not exclusively. In the Year 16 inscription, Nefertiti is "Hmt nsw wrt".

concerned. Since the prenomen of Nefertiti, Ankhkheperure, was of no use to her now and was never intended to be permanent, anyway, Smenkhkare simply adopted it—and became the second "Acencheres" of Manetho.

Regardless, there was now a problem at Akhetaten—a rightful heir and an usurper. It may have followed that certain officials of the dead Akhenaten did not wish to serve Smenkhkare—or he did not want them. If they left or were made to leave the city, their tombs would have been abandoned, too. As it happened, the entire duration of the court at Akhetaten lasted no more than 11-12 years under Neferkheperure Akhenaten and not much longer after his passing. If any of the men who had received the royal boon of a sepulcher from the latter had ever been buried in any one of them, no sign has remained of it. Ay was one of those men and we know he certainly was buried elsewhere and had risen to unexpected heights.

There are some hints that, after Year 12 of Akhenaten, his city might have been visited by a plague, a sickness that perhaps halted work on everything for a time. The Great Plague of London [bubonic] lasted from 1665-66 CE. It killed an estimated 100,000 people in the city of London, 15% of its population. King Charles II, his family and his court, left the city for Salisbury and, when the contagion spread, moved to Oxford. The poor did not have these options and the same pattern may have been seen at Akhetaten, which was in the desert in the first place.[95] The wealthy, including the king, had

---

95 The corpses of many malnourished young people have been

boats to take them elsewhere on the river to anywhere they may have deemed safer. Akhenaten and his family, what was left of it, must have returned, but one cannot say with confidence that this was the case with all the members of his court. Since Meryre, the high priest of the Aten, is attested in Year 16, he had obviously retained his position.

Meryre II, the steward of the house of the queen, Nefertiti, and overseer of the "two treasuries", stayed for a time and recognized the new pharaoh. But perhaps he was also dismissed or fled because the decoration to his tomb stops even before the scene with Smenkhkare and Merytaten could be completed. Not much at all can be stated with certainty even prior to the death of Akhenaten, much less after he was gone.

But Year 12 remains the elephant in the room. Why does it seem like the reign of the heretic pharaoh just screeches to a halt where the decoration is concerned after his Year 12 when he is supposed to have ruled for 17? What happened? Was it really a prolonged plague? A civil war? It is impossible to know.

Tellingly, Nefertiti is referred to, in the Year 12 durbar scene in the tomb of Huya, as "Hmt nsw aAt", which is a title she does not adopt until late in her time, although it does not replace "Hmt nsw wrt". This might indicate that, by Year 12, her coregency with Akhenaten had already ended.

At any rate, a new king arises in Year 17 of Akhenaten. Recently, an attestation of Nefertiti as the queen of Akhenaten in his Year 16 [while many believed

discovered in a commoner cemetery of Akhetaten.

she died earlier] has been announced. Nefertiti was not only there in Year 16, but probably in Year 17, too!

In the durbar scenes, Meryaten is shown as still being a girl but, on the wall with Smenkhkare, she is portrayed as a grown woman. Does this merely reflect her new status—or have five years actually lapsed?

Why were there wine jar dockets with Year 17 partly erased and with a Year 1 surcharged? That was probably because the wine had been placed into the jars in late summer when it ripened, in the 1st month of the first season, Akhet. That the vintage was marked "17" so early in the calendar year indicates, also, that Akhenaten had risen to the kingship coeval with his father's jubilee. Amunhotep III seems to have inaugurated his first heb sed in the 10th month of the year, likely the month of his own accession. And that could explain why the anniversary clock of Akhenaten had already turned by I Akhet [Julian calendar August at the time] because he had become king in II Shomu. For those who can't credit any of this or even a coregency, Manetho has "Amenophis" reigning for 30 years and 10 months. That may be short of the mark for Amunhotep III, but II Shomu still seems to be involved. In that 10th month there arose a succesor—coregency or no.[96]

Scholars have been looking for orderly and sensible answers to the puzzles of the Amarna Era and they can't be blamed. If Smenkhkare, the mystery king, suddenly seems to appear after the durbar, it is easier to assume he was made coregent then. On the other hand,

---

96 Manetho probably had no more means of ascertaining a coregency than we do. But, if he did, does that indicate 30 years alone as king?

Akhenaten was probably still quite a young man in his real Year 12 and it would seem odd that he had already given up having a son of his own by one of his wives. A long gap in the decoration of the tomb of Meryre II is also not easily explained, if Smenkhkare succeeded in Year 17. Still, if he had become a coregent at some earlier time, his own Year 1 would not have been the one substituted for Year 17 on the wine vessel. But I think it was.

It is thought that Smenkhkare's reign lasted no more than a year, but the evidence for such a brief duration is not so secure. He built a large hall, an extension of the Great Palace, for an uncertain purpose, consisting of bricks without straw.[97] For some reason, the new king did not avail himself of the quarries in the vicinity of Akhetaten in order to procure more durable talatat blocks. However, Smenkhkare seems to have commissioned a calcite vase at some point, placing his name next to that of Akhenaten as though he wished to be seen as an appointed and legal successor of the older pharaoh, viewing himself as his son-in-law—which he was, indeed. Or perhaps his widow was responsible for the inscription after the death of her husband. This globular vase was discovered in the tomb of Tutankhamun with cartouches all but erased. Every evidence points to the reign of Smenkhkare, whatever its length, to have been unlawful.

Also, it may be that the usurper had time to

---

97 As Akhetaten was in the desert, there was no straw for the bricks. They contain mainly gravel. Barry Kemp, **The City of Akhenaten and Nefertiti** [London, 2012].

produce two daughters with his wives, named Meryaten-tasherit and Ankhesenpaaten-tasherit. Unless these small girls were twins, born of Queen Merytaten, or the

children of two sisters born in the same year,[98] the new king, Smenkhkare, required more than a year on the throne. But if Smenkhkare was the father of Tutankhaten, the DNA does not allow the daughters of Akhenaten to have been his mother. The mother of Tutankhaten was a princess, regardless, but the daughter of Amunhotep III. It makes sense that, with such a wife, Smenkhkare would not have needed to have Merytaten

---

98 Since Neferneferuaten-tasherit was named for her mother, Nefertiti, it is reasonable to think that all the "juniors" should have been named for their own mothers.

135

for a chief queen.

Since he did have her, it is unlikely that Smenkhkare had already married his own sister. There is

Princesses Neferneferuaten-tasherit, Neferneferure, and Setepenre[99]

the evidence of a wine jar docket from someone's Year I, mentioning "the estate of Smenkhkare, justified" but that Year I could refer to Neferneferuaten or Tutankhaten.

Regardless, Smenkhkare must have died within a brief span because Tutankhaten was able to become pharaoh while still a child. Now came the time for a woman to establish herself as the regent or place-holder

---

99 Line drawings by Norman de Garis Davies are part of this book.

for Tutankhaten, still too young to rule on his own. This was done using the name and epithet "Neferneferuaten, effective for her husband". But who was this royal lady? Most of the evidence points to Nefertiti. After all, the queen had once been a co-king as "Ankhkheperure Neferneferuaten, beloved of [Akhenaten]", but he was no longer alive and it was not thought proper to mention the name of a dead king in the titulary of a living one, even if one was a mere regent and did not expect to continue in this capacity for long. So "husband" had to suffice. The name of Nefertiti is perhaps the most desecrated at Akhetaten, so she may have become persona non grata during the reign of Smenkhkare and had left Akhetaten with her son—taking her majordomo, Meryre II, with her and various other servants.

In fact, the two rivals for supremacy may have been Smenkhkare and Nefertiti, with Tutankhaten not involved due to his age.

A rectangular gray granite base of a statue, now lost, was discovered in a garden in Cairo. The sculpture, probably of Princess Merytaten, once stood at Akhetaten in a sun-shade shrine dedicated to her. A double line of hieroglyphic text is incised on the plinth. Because of the form of the Aten names, the monument must be dated to no later than Year 8 of the rule of Merytaten's father. The inscription of the plinth contains Nefertiti's cartouches, which have been deliberately erased, attesting to her nullification for some reason. Richard Parkinson, in his translation of the glyphs, underlines the erasures:

"May live my father Harakhte rejoicing in his horizon, in his name of Shu

who is in the sun-disk, given life for all time and eternity! The dual-king,

who lives in Truth, Lord of the Two Lands, Neferkheperure-waenre, given

life.....Akhenaten, great in his lifetime; the king's bodily daughter whom he

loves, Meritaten, born of the Great Royal Wife, Neferneferuaten Nefertiti,

*may she live for all time and eternity! Etc....."*100

So here the names of Akhenaten were allowed to remain, but not that of Nefertiti. Moreover, even the dedication on the foot of the late Akhenaten's own coffin, discovered in KV55, seems to have been altered from that of a dialogue between a husband and wife to that of a father and daughter. Bands of text on the lid and trough contain the unique epithets of Akhenaten, "the Perfect Child of the Aten" and "Great in His Lifetime", although, at some later time, his cartouches were excised and the golden face of the coffin partly adzed off. The text on the foot has obviously been carefully altered with application of small pieces of gold plate. Since the alterations include the sun-god Re-Horakhty, whom Akhenaten had banished from the Aten cartouches in Year 9, that king must have been dead when they were made.

The text, as altered, seems to suggest a poignant dialogue between the spirit of a dead king and a surviving daughter, Line 1 through part of 7 being the speech of Akhenaten—and the rest being the response of his daughter, most likely Merytaten, who had previously referred to her father as "Re-Horakhty" on the plinth of

---

100Parkinson, Richard, **Cracking Codes: The Rosetta Stone and Decipherment** [California, 1999]

her statue. After the demise of Akhenaten, there was no compelling reason for Merytaten to avoid any banished names of the Aten, especially since a deceased pharaoh would traditionally have been perceived as "flesh of Re", making his way through the netherworld to some sort of transformation. The dead king would, like the sun-god in the horizon, be born again at dawn. One drawback of the new theology, Atenism, was that it had not apparently developed a funerary cult uniquely its own.

Even though the Osirian epithet of "Maa-kheru" [justified] was dropped from the titles of the deceased during the Amarna period in the tombs of the nobles, it is used in the altered portions of the "prayer" on the foot of the KV55 coffin. In Line 8 of the inscription on the

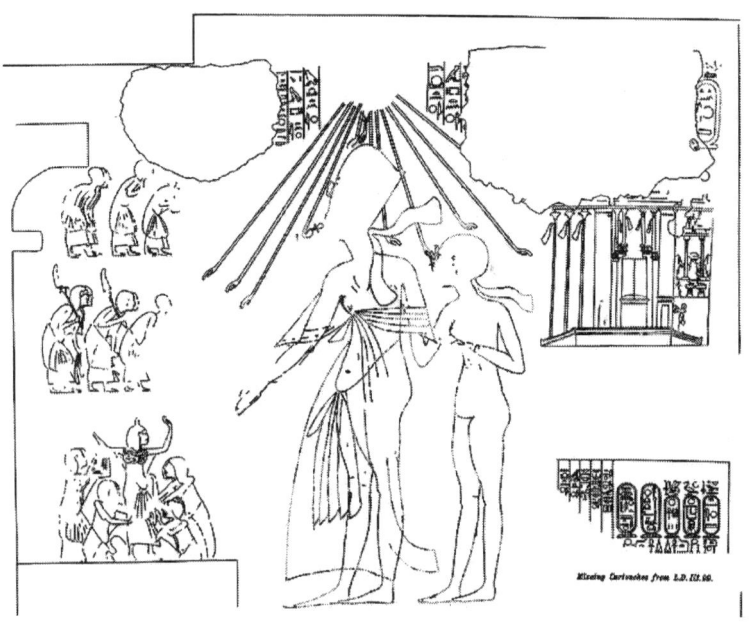

Smenkhkare and Merytaten in the tomb of Meryre II

139

foot of the coffin from KV55, *"my father, Re-Horakhty"* shows the nearby cartouche of Akhenaten as having been later erased and the address changed from "my lord" or "my husband" to "my father" long before. It would appear to me that the usurpation of the throne by the husband of Merytaten had caused a rift between daughter and mother. Their relationship had perhaps even begun to unravel while Akhenaten still lived.

Only with a husband like Smenkhkare did Merytaten have any chance of continuing to be a queen, as she was far too old to become a wife of little Tutankhaten. Regardless, what occurred once Smenkhkare was gone is one of the greatest conundra to emerge from the Amarna Era.

Chapter Seven

PROBLEMS

Later in life, Nefertiti seems to have exchanged her tall, flat-topped blue crown for the more rounded one of the same color seen on the striding statue, below. She appears tired and careworn in this masterwork, her face looking older than a woman of 30 years—which she would have been at the time of the death of her husband—more or less.

The same aging appearance can be perceived in the case of another woman[101] wearing the same crown on a limestone slab. The persons depicted on this plaque have been thought to be Merytaten and Smenkhkare, but Merytaten would have been a very young person, indeed, still a teenager during the time of her marriage. It seems to me, therefore, that the pharaoh with the crippled

---

101 The two ladies, however, must be the same individual due to the crown. Either both are Nefertiti or neither one is.

Nefertiti in the Berlin Egyptian Museum

leg and the queen with the extraordinarily long neck and sagging belly must be Akhenaten and Nefertiti. The relief is not an official portrait of any kind, as in such the ruler would never have been shown using a crutch or lifting a leg in the manner of handicapped persons in Egyptian art. There are none of the obligatory cartouches. It is simply a whimsical piece, perhaps executed at Akhetaten after the death of Neferkheperure. There is no reason to believe that his city was totally abandoned by everyone even after Tutankhamun's move to Memphis was effected. Yet no official portraits can have been fashioned there beyond that time.

On the relief, Nefertiti offers her husband a bouquet of lotus flowers and some yellow mandrake

fruit, which was thought to have aphrodisiacal and healing powers. It was believed that mandrake possessed the ability to cure a number of diseases and even to induce happiness. That is why the roots of mandrake were, at one time, tremendously expensive. The mandrake was used as a sedative, soporific, pain-killller, and also as a treatment for ulceration. We know now why Akhenaten would have been in pain and why he required a crutch. However, the king has a strange expression on his face, so the artist may have intended that mandrake had caused Akhenaten to go into a stupor.

What was surely an authorized likeness is the statue of a very young king Tutankhaten in the Metropolitan Museum of Art.[102] Nothing remains of it now but the head and a hand placed upon it. It has been concluded that the hand must belong to the god, Amun, but the boy-king was not devoted to that god in his earliest years. In my opinion, the delicate, narrow, hand can only be that of a female, the regent for the little pharaoh.

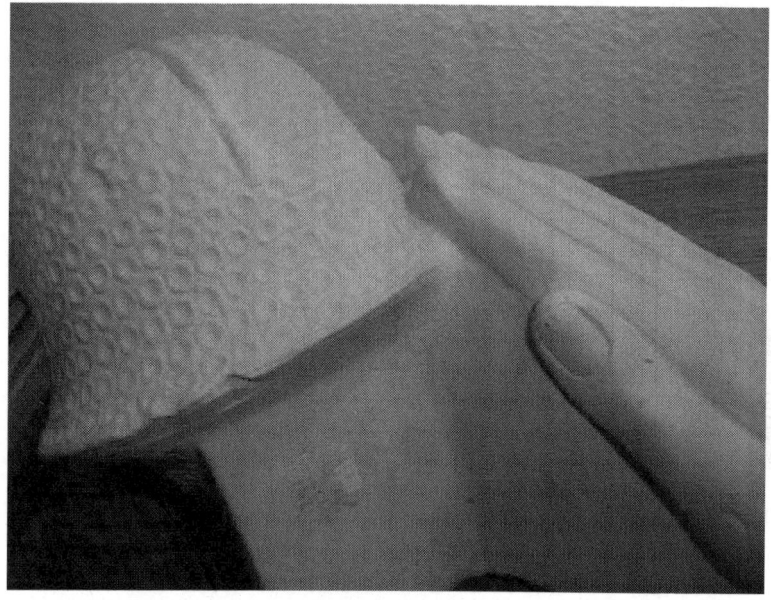

A difficulty, in my view, is that the faces of the golden canopic coffinettes, used for the burial of Tutankhamun, do not resemble Nefertiti at all. But they,

102 The author has an exact, to scale, replica.

too, had previously been inscribed with the name of "Neferneferuaten, effective for her husband". The coffinettes are of the rishi type but wholly evidence a return to polytheistic ways. A pectoral, originally fashioned for Neferneferuaten with the name of Tutankhamun superimposed, features a winged goddess, something one would also not associate with Nefertiti— unless she had decided to return to the old religion at last. Akhenaten would have hated the very idea, but perhaps Nefertiti wisely discerned the theological direction that would be best for safeguarding the throne for her son.

At any rate, we have the hieratic inscription, a graffito from the tomb of Pairi [TT139], written by a priest of the temple of Ankhkheperure, Pawah. It reads [as partially reconstructed]:[103]

"Year 3, third month of Inundation, day 10. The King of Upper and Lower Egypt, Lord of the Two Lands Ankhkheperure Beloved of Aten,[?] the Son of Re Neferneferuaten Beloved of Waenre.[?] Giving worship to Amun, kissing the ground to Wenennefer by the lay priest, scribe of the divine offerings of Amun in the Mansion [temple] of Ankhkheperure in Thebes, Pawah, born to Yotefseneb. He says: ..."

It is a problematic writing because, since it does not refer to Smenkhkare, there must now be a woman-

---

103 Aidan Dodson, in **Amarna Sunset** [page 46], writes that the "beloved of Waenre" is uncertain. One does have difficulty justifying the name of a dead king in the titulary of a living one, especially since one also sees "Effective for her husband" as a substitution for "beloved of Waenre" elsewhere. The nomen Smenkhkare is not attested as being beloved of anyone.

king who, although probably "beloved of the Aten", has offerings made to Amun in her kingdom, as well! Although that appears to coincide with an item like the pectoral, there clearly is no mention of Tutankhamun, the rightful king. Yet, previously, I have pointed out that, if the boy was crowned even at the age of 8, someone else needed to have reigned for three years before him if he was the son of Akhenaten—and 5 years old when he father died. Since there is a cartouche on a sequin that bears the name of Neferneferuaten followed by the "HqA" sign, which denotes "ruler", these are all indications that the small boy still had to wait before the crown was placed on head.

Tutankhaten can certainly have been even younger than 5 when his father, Akhenaten, passed from life, being born sometime between Years 12 and 17. In fact, the painted plaque, already discussed, may have been a witty and wry statement regarding the desperation of Nefertiti, who was still trying to coax another child, the hoped-for male heir, out of her ailing husband with the aid of mandrake, the stimulant. Alternatively, the piece may be hinting that mandrake had done the trick, as the Nefertiti of the new, later, type of crown can have conceived a boy at last, Tutankhaten—even though the queen was far from the enticing creature of previous times, worn out from years of pregnancies [and possible miscarriages or stillbirths] that had resulted in nothing but girls .

I follow the thinking that the baby shown in the royal tomb at the time of the death of Meketaten is that prince. But exactly what year beyond Year 12 Meketaten died cannot be known. Also, the striding statue of Nefertiti at Berlin can actually be representing her as pregnant.

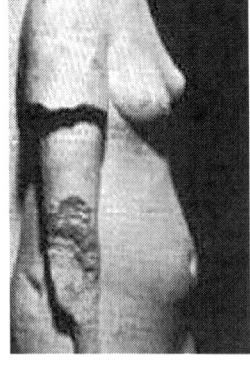

It really does look as if Neferneferuaten has abandoned the dogmatic stance of Akhenaten regarding the worship of the Aten as sole deity. That short period appears to have been officially over in her third year, which must have been during a sole reign and not a coregency—although Year 3 need not have been the precise terminus for her.

It is possible some of the funerary items of Smenkhkare had first been appropriated for Nefertiti, but were later given to Tutankhamun. Quite likely, by then the status of Nefertiti had reverted to dowager queen with pharaonic-appearing canopic coffinettes no longer suitable—or she had simply died as queen regnant but still had no pharaonic funeral, being a mere regent for the true heir.

Regardless, it remains possible that the widowed

Nefertiti, after the death of Smenkhkare, resumed her coregency as Ankhkheperure Neferneferuaten—only this time with her little boy. Just when, if ever, their reigns began to be simultaneous is a problem I cannot solve.

Manetho appears to think that the first "Acencheres" was succeeded by her brother, who lasted 9 years on the throne. Since his name was given as "Rathotis" and not "Acencheres", perhaps the Egyptian historian had someone in mind for whom there was no known prenomen, the then not-at-all famous King Tut—tomb whereabouts unknown and monuments usurped by his successors. By the same token, it would have been difficult for Manetho to know for certain if Tutankhamun was the brother or son of the female ruler.

But an alternative should not be ignored and that is yet another Ankhkheperure Neferneferuaten, a younger one—even Ankhesenpaaten. Indeed, this last was a princess/queen who was at least 6 years older than Tutankhaten, a mere lad.[104] Ankhesenpaaten could have ruled for and with her brother/husband and soon the pair adopted their new names and revived the old religion. To be married to ones little brother may be far from an ideal situation but that was the circumstance of

---

104 Unless she was Ankhesenpaaten-tasherit, instead. The putative wife of Tutankhamun, the mummy known as KV21A, as published in the JAMA paper [DNA study, Hawass et al] cannot be the daughter of the Younger Lady and the KV55 individual and is therefore not a sister of Tutankhamun. However, it is possible, from the few alleles culled from her remains, that KV21A can have been a granddaughter of the parents of Tutankhamun, her father having been someone related to the royal family in some fashion.

Cleopatra VII until Julius Caesar intervened.

On the other hand, Merytaten could have continued for a couple of years after Smenkhkare's death, simply annexing his regnal year. Tutankhaten was Merytaten's little brother, as well, but she reigned without him. However, one would have to find an explanation as to why either of these two queens would have chosen to use the name "Neferneferuaten" which was never associated with either of them, previously. There was Neferneferuaten-tasherit, a younger daughter of Nefertiti, but she was unlikely to have superseded her elder sisters. Exactly who the female ruler was with or before Tutankhaten has no easy answer. With present information alone, no one knows exactly what was happening.

At any rate, young Tutankhaten was crowned as a child amid a shaky political situation in Egypt. His miniature royal insignia, the crook and the flail, were retained and placed into his tomb in the Valley of the Kings as a souvenir of those strange times. Tutankhamun's own Restoration Stela claims the land was in turmoil before he assumed the throne and it stands to reason that any loyal surviving women of his immediate family would not have allowed such a vulnerable individual to rule on his own. The fact that Egyptologists find it so frustrating may be a clue that the Amarna era and aftermath was more chaotic than has been suspected.

And, yet, even chaos is governed by mathematics. Time imposes its own order. The following consists of rather tedious but important considerations:

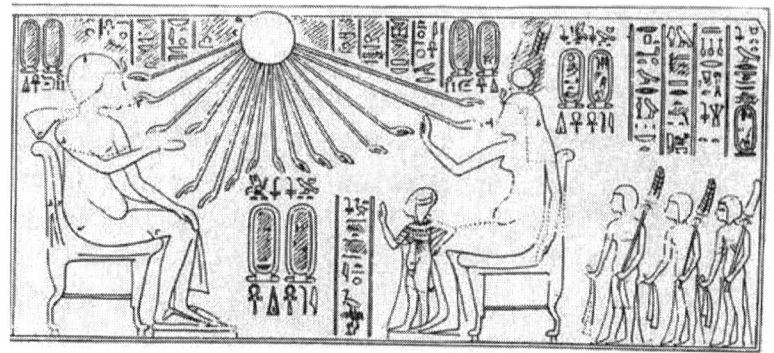

Queen Tiye and Baketaten greeting image of Amunhotep III [tomb of Huya, majordomo of Tiye]. The king is made to appear still alive.

Once more, if Tutankhaten was a minimum of 8 years old upon his accession [with Smenkhkare and/or someone else reigning for 3 years before him] and he was born in Year 12 or 13 of Akhenaten, **if his father was Smenkhkare**—then the latter would have to have been 14 years old at the time to fit to the aging criterion of Derry and Strouhal. 14+8=22. This is now clear. It would mean that, in order for Smenkhkare to have been a son of Amunhotep III and Queen Tiye, he would have had to have been born shortly before Akhenaten was made king. If there was no coregency between Akhenaten and his father, then here was a son born of a man who was soon to die at the age of around 50 and his wife, who was about 45.

Queen Tiye appears at Akhetaten in the tomb of her stewart, Huya. Moreover, the child, Baketaten, accompanies the royal lady in every scene. There are no princes depicted anywhere, except perhaps in a mourning scene in the Amarna royal tomb. However, the presence of little Princess Baketaten at Akhetaten appears to indicate that Tiye and Amunhotep III were still having children in their middle-age. I do not believe the little girl was the product of incest. Even Aldred, who thought a 12-year coregency was best, did not believe one should read too much into that relief on the north wall lintel, tomb of Huya. There Amunhotep III sits as casually and, apparently, as much alive as Akhenaten

Banquet scene with Akhenaten, Nefertiti, two princessses, and the queen mother with Baketaten sitting at her side [tomb of Huya]

does on the other side of the lintel. He makes a kind of "blessing" gesture toward his queen and Baketaten and they greet him in return. However, a tomb being a "mansion of eternity", the lines between life and death, then and now, can become blurred.

All a coregency can do is alter the ages of Amunhotep III and Queen Tiye when their son, the future Akhenaten, was made a co-king [younger, and in the case of Amenhotep III, still living].   But the same number of years have to pass in the kingship of Akhenaten, regardless. Time goes by in the same fashion whether kings rule simultaneously or alone. Akhenaten used his own count.

If Smenkhkare's putative mother, Queen Tiye, died in Year 14 of Akhenaten, Smenkhkare would have been only about 15 years old at the time. **But Queen Tiye would have died at the age of 60 without a co-regency.** It was possible for her to have a son of that age—but impossible for Tiye to have had Baketaten, a tiny girl.[105]

In the tomb of Huya, Baketaten is shown much smaller on one side of the lintel than Merytaten, the eldest daughter of Akhenaten, on the opposite side. One must recall that all these decorations were likely made prior to Year 12—so even Merytaten can only have been somewhat less than 12 years old then. [The names of the Aten indicate the scenes post-date Year 9.]

With even eight years of coregency, Tiye can have had one final child with Amunhotep III, who was still quite small in Year 12 of their son, Akhenaten.   By this time, of course, Amunhotep III was dead and Tiye and Baketaten living at Akhetaten.   If so, where was Smenkhkare, still a youth, himself, in Year 12 of his brother?   Who was caring for the other living daughters

---

105 The average age of the menopause in modern Egyptian women is 46.7 years. Lower bone mineral density makes them more vulnerable to osteoporosis than their Western counterparts. **Climacteric**, 2006, Vol. 9, No. 6 : Pages 421-429, "Menopause in Egypt: past and present perspectives", Dr. H. Sallam. A.F. Galal, A. Rashed.

of Nebmaare Amunhotep, whatever their ages, and where?[106] These are questions seldom asked, so great is the concentration on the mysteries of life at Akhetaten.

Even if Tutankhaten had been born after Akhenaten had died and in the sole reign of Smenkhkare, the problems do not disappear. Smenkhkare Djeserkheperu still has to be between 22 and 25 when he died in order to be the KV55 individual, according to the

Akhenaten, Nefertiti, and daughters headed by Merytaten [tomb of Huya]

age limits set by Derry and Strouhal—those very limits that supposedly ruled out Akhenaten as being the man found in KV55. Smenkhkare would have been only 14 when Akhenaten died in order to be 22 when his son was 8 in this scenario. He would have been younger than his queen, Merytaten, who would have been about 17 at the end of her father's life.

Crucially, without a coregency, Amunhotep III can never have been the father of Smenkhkare under these

---

106 Probably at Medinet Gurob, a royal estate known to contain a harem.

circumstances, as he would have been deceased before Smenkhkare was born. Also, for Tutankhaten to have become king at even the age of 8, a much longer reign for Smenkhkare is mandated —of which there is absolutely no proof. The older Tutankhaten was when he took the throne, the worse this scenario gets.

Yet another version of the script does not depend on how old Smenkhkare was when Tutankhaten became pharaoh because Smenkhkare would have died within the reign of his brother, Akhenaten, as a co-king. Let us imagine the unlikely occasion of Akhenaten creating a male coregent around his Year 12, a younger full brother to whom he gave his eldest daughter, Merytaten, for a bride. Probably, by then, Merytaten would have been as old as 12 and considered the right age to be a real wife to someone.

By age 13, she can have given birth to a child, but the DNA says that the KV55 individual and the Younger Lady are a full brother and sister and, therefore, the female cannot be Merytaten. This would mean that, if Smenkhkare's remains were found in KV55, he, as the father of Tutankhamun, sired him with another royal princess at the same time he was supposed to be married to Akhenaten's very young daughter, his chief queen! How many wives did this Smenkhkare have? One might say—why can't Baketaten have been a wife of Smenkhkare? She could have been his full sister. But it is doubtful that Princess Baketaten can have been old enough to bear a child by the time Tutankhaten should have been born if he became king at the age of eight or nine years. If Baketaten was even as old as six in Year 12

154

of Akhenaten, then she would only have been eleven when that pharaoh died.

Moreover, at this very time, the younger brother—if that is what Smenkhkare was—would have needed to be not that much younger than Akhenaten, himself. That is because, it being concluded that the co-regent did not live very long, he would have died at age 23, according to Douglas Derry, between 19-22 in the estimation of Eugen Strouhal—and at **least** 24 years old as figured by Professor G. E. Smith. It would have been most unusual [and rather dangerous] for a king of Egypt to have a male/brother coregent who was of his own generation. Even if he had fallen very ill and did not know if he would recover, it seems far more reasonable and much safer for Akhenaten to have appointed his own wife as a co-king. Such a woman, who already had several daughters [who could succeed their father, if necessary], seems a much more reliable interim executive partner.

All things considered, it is far more logical for the KV55 individual to be Akhenaten and the Younger Lady to be Queen Nefertiti. And to admit that we have no idea just who Smenkhkare Djeserkheperu was.

It has been reasoned that, because Amunhotep III and Tiye had been married for so many years, their eldest surviving son, Amunhotep, must have been at least 20 when it was his turn to become the pharaoh. That makes a certain amount of sense, to be sure, but, if Amunhotep IV had been that old he, himself, should have been married for some years. However, at Karnak in the Hut Benben, there is only a single princess following her mother, Nefertiti, at first——and then Meketaten was added, it being conjectured from certain indications that she was not born until Year 4. On the boundary stelae at Akhetaten, there are only Merytaten and Meketaten by Year 5. That would seem to be very few children for a king of about 25, whose main goal should have been the continuation of his family line with the birth of an heir.

The end of the 18th Dynasty was portrayed as being mighty at the time by its artisans. Modern writers have hyped it as being glorious, with references to "Sun Kings". But, by now, it should be apparent that the reality was different from the propaganda. The royal family was, in a word, "pathetic".

Amunhotep III had inherited an empire and he seems to have been a canny ruler. Probably he didn't lack intelligence. That he was influential and the head of a great and powerful nation cannot be doubted. Foreign kings and princes wished to be on good terms with him and wrote to him frequently. However, they sent emissaries, as well, who must have seen or heard something of the truth of matters in the palace. The mighty pharaoh of Egypt and his queen were hardly taller than children. Queen Tiye appeared attractive enough but the great man, himself, was in poor condition in every sense. Nothing magnificent about him at all except perhaps for his attitude. His consort certainly compensated for her tiny stature with an extremely haughty cast of features. Both the king and queen were chubby, especially His Majesty. What stories these envoys must have brought back with them from the court of dreaded Egypt!

The father of Amunhotep III, Thutmose IV, had been a handsome man, whose beauty was acclaimed even while he lived. That king had a smaller version of the jutting, curved noses of his immediate predecessors, Amunhotep II and Thutmose III. But Nebmaare Amunhotep was so unlike them in appearance that one must wonder whom he actually did resemble with his turned-up nose and small chin.

The successor and his own queen looked quite normal. They were not tall, certainly, but many in the known world were no taller. The face of the new king of Egypt appeared more Asiatic than Egyptian. He was running to fat, but at least was not barrel-shaped as his father had been. The pharaoh could be described, but the queen of Egypt defied description. Her wonderful

Tiye and Amunhotep III [Roemer- Pelizaeus-Museum, Hildesheim]

beauty was surely legendary far and wide in her own lifetime.

No one knew what to make of Neferkheperure Akhenaten. Whatever else he was, the young man was still an emperor. The petty princes of the Near East, his vassals, needed him to be strong for his own sake and theirs—but he either wouldn't or couldn't do anything to save the Egyptian empire from those who had designs upon it. Desperate letters to the pharaoh, written on clay tablets in cuneiform, were evidently archived but not much acted upon. Akhenaten ended in disgrace and future kings did their best to wipe out the very memory of him. If only they could have realized the futility of their efforts!

This king was not without his physical problems. His teeth were good, he had a mild cleft palate that probably didn't bother him, but he had an osteoma in the maxillary sinus. This, too, may have been asymptomatic, but it had the potential to cause facial pain, swelling, and nasal discharge. Akhenaten, young as he was, probably walked with a pronounced limp and certainly needed a crutch. During his examination by the experts in Cairo, he was diagnosed with bone fibroma and femoral osseous collapse. It means the man had a bad hip. Osteonecrosis of the hip develops when the blood supply to the femoral head is disrupted. Lacking adequate nourishment, the bone in the head of the femur dies and gradually collapses. The result is that the cartilage covering the hip bones also collapses, and one gets disabling arthritis. In a youthful individual, the process can have begun with an injury. Once again, the chariot can be suspected as the potentially hazardous vehicle, just as it has been in the case of Tutankhamun.

In our time, Akhenaten is somewhat famous outside the realm of Egyptology, but that is partly due to Nefertiti and her marvelous limestone bust, the icon of beauty that few fail to recognize. Her husband is mostly lauded for being the first monotheist in the history of the world.

Akhenaten was, indeed, a monotheist to the extent that his existence as an ancient Egyptian and a pharaoh allowed him to be. He reasoned, quite accurately, of course, that there could be no life without the sun, which rose every morning without fail and bestowed its benefices upon the earth. Some believe that a phenomenon, perhaps a lengthy solar eclipse, instilled a fear in the heart of the young Amunhotep that perhaps the sun was sending an ominous message that it was displeased and might not be so predictably generous with its life-giving rays in the future.[107] Therefore, Akhenaten soon dedicated his life to adoring and propitiating the solar disc. He is seen raising his arms to those of the Aten even at Karnak, prior to Year 5.

How did Akhetaten become fixated on the solar disc? Either he ceased to have confidence in the reliability of the sun [and also, in his egotism, felt he was the man who could keep it shining if he paid it sufficient attention] or he thought the Aten was the supreme god,

107The total eclipse that could be viewed in Egypt and happened on May 14, 1338 BCE would mandate a very low chronology for the reign of Akhenaten and his predecessors. As matters stand, I think the time line should be raised due to the certainty of a coregency between Amunhotep III and Akhenaten.

but a jealous one who brooked no rivals. Or perhaps Akhenaten had grown to be an anti-theist, had no confidence in the Egyptian pantheon at all. There are some people who are skeptical by their very nature. But a king of Egypt could not rule without at least one god. Without the title "sA ra" or "son of the sun", he was just as human as anyone else—and that would not do. Moreover, the usefulness and power of the brilliant Aten was obvious to all.

Amun, whose name means "hidden" was, of course, nowhere to be seen except in the form of an idol—which could be manipulated by men to do their bidding. This god had a powerful priesthood and one had to be wary of its chief servitor, the very man who could claim any kind of oracle had been handed down by Amun, if it suited him.

If Akhenaten was going to live far from Thebes, not in the palace at Malkata, as his father had done, the dissolution of the worship of Amun was not an unwise move. Events in the distant future of Egypt would prove that the high priest of that deity was capable of setting himself up as an authority, rivaling even the pharaoh, who also resided a long way from Thebes. By that time, at the end of Dynasty 20, the kings of Egypt probably even spoke a different dialect from the southerners, they had lived in the Northland for so long.

As for the veneration of gods in animal form, in outlawing this Akhenaten showed himself to be progressive. Lest one be tempted to think that the veneration of animals, which is what many of the established deities basically were, is totally harmless if unsophisticated, one must be reminded that such a theology can sometimes cause difficulties. The ancient writers have informed us that the worship of the sacred cats of Egypt posed a serious threat, as anyone suspected of harming one was put to death by the ordinary people around him. Even a cat that died of natural causes was supposedly mourned by the Egyptians by the act of shaving off their own eyebrows. Feeding stray cats can cause an over-population of the same and they can easily become carriers of bubonic plague or *Yersinia pestis* in hot, dry areas. This usually happens when an infected rodent either bites or is bitten by a cat. Sometimes the feline can pass the plague onto a human.

The museums of the world possess mummies of the various creatures held sacred in ancient Egypt. Hundreds of them have been found. Their cults were evidently very popular, a way of life. The ban on venerating animals dedicated to certain gods lasted for only the blink of an eye and, then, was resumed with as much enthusiasm as before.

Akhenaten, evidently, decided that all this fuss over zoomorphic gods was useless, even ridiculous, and put an end to it. Bast, Anubis, Thoth—the entire animal-headed pantheon was officially no more. The only animal allowed in his theology was the Mnevis bull of Heliopolis, as he was associated with the solar cult. The burial of the bull would now take place at Akhetaten, the new center of the worship of the sun. And, of course, the cobra remained upon the brow of the king, but that was merely a symbol of the fact that he was a dreaded ruler.

162

Boundary stela and statues of the royal family.

One could not do away with everything because the nature of kingship had to remain inviolate. If the pharaoh happened to be so unfortunate as to be an invalid who had difficulty just living his life, let alone dealing with the complexities of overseeing an empire, that did not matter. He occupied the throne as a relative of the gods [or a single god], reigning by divine right.

Chapter Eight

PROPAGANDA

At some point after a boy of around eight or nine became king of Egypt on his own, whoever was the real power behind the throne decided to erect a stela in the Great Hypostyle Hall in front of the Third Pylon of the Temple of Amun at Karnak. The incised text hinted to the prophets, priests, and whoever else could read the writing on the slab that, if the harvest failed or the land did not otherwise prosper, it was not the fault of the present administration. Because it had disassociated itself with any recent reigns that might have gone before.

True, the new king, Nebkheperure Tutankhamun, was the son of one of them, had to be—but, on the Restoration Stela, he has no father save Amun although, of course, Son of the Sun was part of the titulary formula. The new ruler was referred to as "the glorious seed, the sacred egg"...."begotten by Amun, himself". This sort of hyperbole was not exactly new in the time of the 18ᵗʰ Dynasty, but it came in handier at this time than ever before because Tutankhamun's real father had to be painted out of the picture entirely.

Much of the text alludes to the displeasure of the gods at the havoc the previous, anonymous, pharaohs had wrought. No wonder, as their temples had become abandoned, their halls footpaths. No offerings were made and so the deities had turned their backs on Egypt and nothing good came of anything.

I do not think it is just a coincidence that the stela is dated Year 1, 4th month of the season of Akhet [Khoiak] Day 19. In 1331 BCE, a reasonable date for the "restoration of the old order", this amounted to the 7th of November [Julian calendar]. By this time the annual Nile flood had receded and it was the time of sowing. Since the stela mentioned some things Tutankhamun had already fashioned for the gods, new and better statues, shrines, new servitors for their temples, they should now be propitiated. He had spared no expense. If the height of the flood hadn't quite been up to expectation, if the harvest should be less than abundant—well, this king was not to blame. He had done all he could to curry favor with the old gods—or at least that was what the Thebans were given to know.

The ruler was not to be seen. He was far away in the Northland, at Memphis, living in the palace of his illustrious forebear, Thutmose I. No harm in mentioning the name of that king. It might lend the impression that Tutankhamun had it in mind to emulate that great conqueror, whose heart had certainly not been weak in his body. The stela admits the sovereign is young but he is advanced in every way. He is knowledgeable like Ra, ingenious like Ptah, and as perceptive as Thoth. Never mind that he is only a child and the victim of incest in some ways best not to mention. He is working in the best interests of the nation and the rest is up to the gods, themselves. Evidently, a successor of Tutankhamun, Horemheb, found the Restoration Stela expressed his opinion of all those rulers who had come before *him*, Tutankhamun included. And so he usurped that slab as soon as he was able.

Actually, in his Year 1, **Tutankhaten** should have been still an Atenist king—and not in Memphis with his later nomen. The Restoration Stela is a contradiction of the golden throne discovered in KV62, which shows the boy crowned with the Atef, his old name of Tutankhaten remaining visible on the chair. Therefore, since the throne evidences the new name on the front, it is obvious that it was fashioned for someone named Tutankhaten but altered—and that the queen shown with him on the item had originally been called by another name, as well. Can this change really have occurred within the space of a single year?

If not, then one must suspect that the Restoration Stela existed to wipe out the memory of "Tutankhaten", as well as Akhenaten, and can never have been erected in Year 1. Was it nothing but an anachronistic piece of propaganda? Not only could it erase the true beginning of the kingship of Tutankhamun, but his real father and the woman who had served as regent for him, as well. Tutankhaten had to be reinvented completely. That he

167

had probably been born at Akhetaten would have to become a secret, too, as the god Amun, who had sired him, had never existed there. Just as the legitimizing texts of Hatshepsut were meant to convince future generations that she was a rightful ruler instead of an usurper, the Restoration Stela, too, may have had the mission of re-writing history. Tutankhamun had been born at the holy city where Amun reigned supreme, perhaps at the pleasant site of Armant, about 12 miles south of Thebes. Yes, why not? No matter where he resided for the rest of his reign, the king would have the title of Ruler of the Southern On, meaning Armant.

Tutankhamun is called "King Tut" in the familiar sort of way one would refer to an old school chum. He has become part of the pop culture. We are used to him; he has always been with us because most of us were born long after 1922—while simultaneously not knowing him at all. Judging by the contents of his tomb, this unlucky young king was rich beyond imagining. Many people take for granted that Tutankhamun only had one wife, Ankhesenamun, but the tomb of his Viceroy of Kush, named Huy, exists to demonstrate this was not so. The decoration of TT40 centers around a momentous occasion, the reception by the young monarch of the tribute of the southern lands, which includes, of course, gold. With the precious metal comes the assurance that more will not be difficult to procure in the form of a bride for Tutankhamun, a daughter of a ruler of one of the countries south of Egypt proper.

Besides being young, what sort of king was

Tutankhamun in reality? Due to the magnificent work of goldsmiths and sculptors of his reign, we see him as a beautiful boy and young man. It appears that the king really did inherit some of his mother's good looks—but

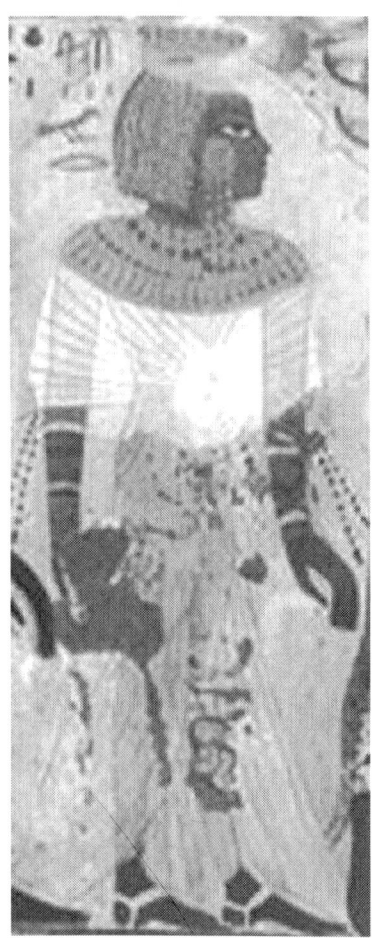

Bringing of a Nubian bride for Tutankhamun, possibly the daughter of Heqanefer, who had an Egyptian name
[tomb of Huy]

the fact remains that Tutankhamun was the product of incest. Nobody realized it or actually wanted to imagine this until the DNA testing revealed the truth. Some don't want to believe it now. Even after the results were published—child of a full brother and sister—people are still making arguments that this cannot be so.

In that same publication of the DNA analysis, the opinions of other experts regarding the physical problems of the king were included. In addition to having a severe form of malaria and possibly fatal trauma to the knee and sternum, Tutankhamun's body evidences things that could be associated with his inbreeding, such as a cleft palate and mild club foot. Walking must have been extremely difficult because the king also suffered from Freiberg-Kohler syndrome [juvenile aseptic bone necrosis], meaning the bones of his foot were dying and collapsing. It is hardly a wonder that 130 sticks or canes were found in Tutankhamun's tomb.

It can't be diagnosed with radiological imaging, but Tutankhamun may also have been mentally deficient. The children of incest are not always retarded, yet studies have shown that the odds are good that they can be. In a modern Czechoslovakian survey, it was seen that fewer than half of the children whose parents were closely related were completely healthy. In the cases of first degree incest [such as a brother with a sister] 40% of the offspring were born with either autosomal recessive disorders, congenital physical defects, or severe intellectual shortcomings. Another 14 % of the children in the study had mild retardation.

Did the handsome effigies of the young pharaoh

170

create a feeling of reassurance among those able to view these statues that a young and virile ruler with a conservative viewpoint was seated on the throne—never indicating for a moment that the pharaoh was nothing but a half-wit?[108] We will likely never know the truth of the matter now but, at the time, there were those who knew only too well, of course. Horemheb, a future king, was a very important official in the administration of Tutankhamun. In a biographical narrative on a monument in the Turin Museum, he states that he was summoned to the palace to mollify someone who, in modern parlance, was "having a fit". This may hint at some recurring problem but, of course, on the king's own monuments he was a paragon.

Perhaps in the beginning it was not yet so obvious that there was something more seriously wrong with the little king than one had ever observed in his father or grandfather. For the sake of poor King Tut, who already had or would soon have multiple physical defects, one hopes that he was at least of normal intelligence. One would have liked him to have made a positive impression during the few years that he was fated to grace the earth. Even I, who have no romantic illusions about the kings of Egypt, can't help but feel a certain compassion toward this ill-fated youth whose great wealth availed nothing in the end, even though he was able to "take it with him" to some extent. Moreover, if the age-at-death assigned to the Younger Lady, who is probably Nefertiti and

---

108 It is my opinion that the so-called "reconstructions" of the face of Tutankhamun are entirely useless. Since his ancient portraits mostly agree, we know how he looked.

171

Tutankhamun's mother, is correct—the boy had become an orphan while still a child. Had she not died at around the age of 35, Neferneferuaten would probably have extended her regency as Tutankhamun was really not yet of an age to rule alone.

Egyptologists are not given to expressing admiration for the ancient subjects of their research. They know better, and leave breathless enthusiasm to the Egyptophiles, the ones who desire a politically correct picture of the past. These tend to get rather upset if one happens to suggest that their favorite pharaoh, who appears rather scary as a mummy, was probably a lot more scary in life to his servants and subjects.

Personally, I tend to think that, judging by the majority of the eastern potentates over the centuries, the pharaohs were probably mostly tyrants who gave themselves a good press via their official fictions. [Tyrants, of course, are not limited to the East.] When primogeniture is the rule for succession, there will naturally be some not-very-bright heirs. I am not sure actual imbeciles were considered—unless perhaps it was a case of the last surviving son of the direct line of rulers.

Incest has always been a taboo in most populations for rather obvious reasons. That the ancient Egyptian royals were ignorant of its ill effects on the children can scarcely be credited. The land of Egypt was, among its neighbors in all directions, renowned for its wisdom and know-how. As for science, one cannot expect that the Egyptians understood, for example, that microbes caused disease because microbes are invisible to the naked eye. However, the potential for harm in consanguinity was well known even by the illiterate in various cultures when the earth was still considered to be flat. In a story from the Late Period of Egyptian history, a prince and a princess fell in love but their father, the pharaoh, thought it far better that they should marry others.

"It is you who distress me. If it so happens that I have only two children, is it right to marry the one to the other? I will marry Naneferkaptah to the daughter of a general, and I will marry Ahwere to the son of another general so that our family may increase!"[109]

So exactly why the parents of Nebkheperure Tutankhamun, another prince and princess, became a couple is not clear. Can it have been for religious reasons? Did Amunhotep III actually identify with the sun-god to the point of wanting a Shu and a Tefnut as his heirs, the children of his body? Were such fanciful and superstitious absurdities able to overrule all common sense? Anyone who views religion with a clear eye knows only too well that it is mostly based on believing things that go against better judgment, a phenomenon that persists in the face of advanced scientific knowledge and mind-boggling technology. In my opinion, this is one of the greatest weaknesses of the human species—this

---

109 *"Setne Khaemwas and Naneferkaptah"*, translation by Miriam Lichtheim in **Ancient Egyptian Literature, Vol. III** [London, 1980] The prince and princess were able to overcome their father's objections. Lichtheim rendered a word as "increase" and that may have been the best choice. As I do not have the Demotic text, I do not know, but the implication is nevertheless clear that such unions could prevent the dynasty from "flourishing" or cause it to become too feeble to continue. That certainly was the case with Tutankhamun.

endless need to believe in ideas and dogmas of which no proof has ever existed and to feel insulted when ones faith is questioned.

Therefore, yes—one cannot exclude that the royal family suffered from delusions that even modern persons of faith would find illogical—although they were just a variation on the same old theme of belief in the impossible.

Tutankhaten/amun required a chief queen, one which he was surely too young to choose for himself when he first arose to the kingship. Her name was Ankhesenamun, as we know, but, if she was really the full sister of the young pharaoh, it would have spelled certain disaster for any offspring. This would have been a case of first degree incest twice over and to have permitted it would seem a great stupidity even for a family steeped in the superstitious beliefs that went along with pharaoh as god. Tutankhamun's sister, Ankhesenpaaten the elder, would have been some years older than her brother. But Ankhesenpaaten-tasherit would have been about the same age as the boy king.

However, to have married her, instead of the older princess, would not have been any wiser—especially if her father was Akhenaten and the mother was Ankhesenpaaten the elder. With that much consanguinity, it is unlikely any children can have survived. Somewhat better would have been an Ankhesenpaaten whose parents were Smenkhkare and the elder Amarna princess of that name. At least Smenkhkare **might** have introduced some new blood, as he was not necessarily the son of Amunhotep III and

174

Queen Tiye if he is not the KV55 individual. In that event, Tutankhamun would have a consort who was only his niece instead of a sister.

Thus far, the Cairo DNA study appears to indicate the latter scenario—although the case is not yet closed as far as I am concerned. Regardless, Tutankhamun had no living children that we know of and certainly no surviving son.

Tutankhamun pouring ointment into the hand of his queen, Ankhesen-amun. He also, significantly, appears to hold mandrake fruits.

But he had parents, and there is evidence that he did not forget Akhenaten, his father, in reality—no matter what the propaganda would have people believe. KV55 was closed with the seal of Nebkheperure Tutankhamun, orginally. It was he [or whoever ran the country in his name] who brought the father from Amarna to the Theban necropolis to be interred with his predecessors. How many of the family of Tutankhamun ended up in KV55 is difficult to know for certain, but Akhenaten ultimately was discovered alone in the 20th Century CE. Probably, when the tomb was entered in the time of the 19th Dynasty, any companions of the heretic were distanced from his unholy presence—perhaps moved to KV35 then.[110] Since Nefertiti was not in KV55, this may have been because she had initiated the reversion to orthodoxy, or at least permitted religious freedom. Or, for all we know, Nefertiti had no wish to be interred with her late husband at all and she, Queen Tiye, and the prince had first been laid in WV22, the tomb of Amunhotep III. There was an enigmatic graffito discovered on a wall of this tomb, reading "Year 3, III Akhet, day 7", which was perhaps the day in the reign of Tutankhamun when the move was made. Regardless, the question remains—what became of the coffins of this trio, their shabtis, etc?[111]

It must have been sometime after the death of Tutankhamun that the cartouches of Akhenaten were removed from his coffin, although it was not robbed of whatever gold it contained. The mummy also retained jewelry, although it wasn't of the first quality—with the exception of a beautiful collar that contained, among other elements, those in the shape of the "nfr" glyph.

---

110 Akhenaten's figure was also erased from the funerary shrine of Queen Tiye in KV55.

111 Although some items exist that probably came from the burial of the former crown prince, Thutmose, if he is the KV35YP.

Although the golden face of the coffin was mutilated, it seems to have been the work of officials and not robbers. Akhenaten was intended to become a nonentity after his death. No one could have foreseen that his unique epithets, "great in his lifetime" and "the perfect child of the Aten" would make the king instantly recognizable to scholars thousands of years into the future. Nor could anyone have envisioned that all the excoriation would prove futile—but the very thing that no one cared about, which was Akhenaten's youth, would prove the obstacle to his bones being identified in another age.

Precisely why Akhenaten has been viewed as a middle-aged man when he died is difficult to say. He may have been intelligent [perhaps] but he certainly was not wise. Nothing he did as a king of Egypt can be construed as successful. Even the city which he built soon became a ghost town not only on account of what it represented, but because it was not very well situated as far as resources were concerned. Not only were ordinary people malnourished at Akhetaten [probably having been forced to migrate there] but they were depicted in the oppressive stance of bowing from the waist. This, also, says something about Akhenaten and how he viewed and/or treated his servants. Most likely he was hardly a beloved ruler. Even though he took pains to have himself portrayed as a doting father and loving husband, he may still have been a cruel man. Or perhaps merely an inept, impractical one—we simply cannot know the truth.[112]

---

112 Barry Kemp has noted that a prevalence of young people, teens, pre-

Scholars do not much go in for characterizing the rulers of Egypt as having any certain type of personality as that is hard to gather from hagiographic sources. Some of them have been called "great" but that also can be called into question. For example, Thutmose III has been equated with Napoleon Bonaparte. True, both were conquerors, but the latter spilled a great deal of blood, including that of Frenchmen, and the former was probably the biggest thief the ancient Egyptians had ever heard of. Year after year, he went east, seizing as much of the crops of others that he thought could logically be carried back to Egypt, in addition to other things of value. People lost their freedom and were taken to the land of the conqueror as slaves. Fruit trees were cut down, leaving the indigenous populations even less to eat. Regardless, Thutmose III was interested in botany, which makes his lack of regard for the trees seem odd.

The Egyptians probably didn't mind the ways of their king, but the peoples to the east of Egypt must have dreaded the mention of the name of Menkheperre Thutmose for he literally took the bread out of the mouths of children. Very likely, he learned ruthlessness from a real master—or rather a mistress.

---

teens, and children, were discovered in a cemetery near the North Tombs at Tell el Amarna. One way of devastating ones supposed enemies was to carry off their children. Prior to the time of the Spanish Inquisition, in 1485, about 2,000 Portuguese Jewish youths and children were deported to the island of São Tomé off the coast of Africa, where most died of the harsh conditions while forced to work in the sugar fields. Meanwhile, one attempted to convert them to Catholicism. It may have happened that Akhenaten took these children to his desert city as hostages against attack by any powerful potential rebels within Egypt or without.

The truth about Hatshepsut is not very pretty, but try telling that to her multitude of "fans". She is an ancient Joan of Arc, the first feminist, "beautiful", a wise "teacher" of Thutmose III—in other words everything but the overreaching, clever liar that the archaeological evidence points to as being the reality. Despite what research has uncovered, the propaganda of Hatshepsut continues to be believed by those who "love Egypt" but who can't be bothered to look closely at all the evidence.

King Ay, the successor of Tutankhamun, has truly been taken to task in the past few decades, even accused of being a murderer, but he was probably no worse than the other opportunists of the earlier part of the dynasty—to which he may have been related in some fashion, for all we know.

Recently, a CT scan of the mummified remains of young King Tutankhamun showed that a slow, lingering death was possible due to a severe knee-cap injury which might have become infected. At any rate, the pharaoh appears to have died of some kind of trauma and may even have gone into a coma, leaving no one at Egypt's helm. That this situation was quickly remedied, however, seems to be indicated by a scene in KV62, the tomb of the pharaoh.

There Ay, already crowned with the khepresh, performs the "opening of the mouth" ceremony on a depiction of Tut as Osiris. This is an unprecedented portrayal of the successor as king in a royal tomb and, in my opinion, strongly suggests that Ay had become coregent prior to the demise of Tutankhamun. When the

179

cartouches of co-regnant kings are together, one of them is usually styled "nb irt xt"—and that is the case in Kv62. Because, once sealed, it was not expected—or at least hoped—that anyone would enter the king's tomb again, it is not likely that Ay had himself portrayed as the new ruler for propaganda purposes. He was merely shown performing the ritual in a capacity in which he had already been serving before the death of Tutankhamun and could no longer be depicted as a commoner sans diadem.

Since Tutankhamun ruled for nine to ten years, probably dying in the 10th, it stands to reason that his tomb had already begun to be excavated. However, the small KV62 hardly evidences years of work. That is why scholars of the past, even though they did not see a coregency of the successor, postulated that Ay took the larger tomb of the young king for himself and had another excavated for Tutankhamun where he could even insert his own image. There is no reason why Tutankhamun, the ruler of the return to the orthodox religion, should not have opted for a burial in the West Valley, where the last great pharaoh prior to the Atenist supremacy was interred—namely Amunhotep III. Therefore, WV23, the ultimate royal tomb of Ay, may have originally been intended for Nebkheperure Tutankhamun.

It is indicated, also, that both KV62 and WV23 had been painted by the same outline-artist , the poorly executed, even cartoonish, images are so alike. Apes figure prominently in both tombs. However, in the case of WV23, this artist seems to have been a bit confused as to how he should decorate this tomb for Ay. It is difficult to know why WV23 ended up a kind of compromise between a royal tomb and that of a commoner, including elements not normally seen in a kingly burial. So perhaps it had belonged to the powerful Ay from the beginning and had merely been altered to provide for his ultimate kingly status. In the aftermath of his brief reign, Ay's images were simply hacked away by a totally unsentimental someone, leaving only one "ka figure" which was let alone on account of respect for royal ancestors fused into this ka [per Nicholas Reeves].

Various irregularities at the end of the reign of the unfortunate Tutankhamun certainly exist, not the least of which is the action of his widow writing to the king of the Hittites, petitioning for a prince to become her husband and ruler of Egypt beside her.

Many have doubted that the writer was Queen Ankhesenamun, but it is a plain fact that only the prenomen of Tutankhamun, Nebkheperure, truly fits to the "Nibhurryia" [or Bibhurriya] written in cuneiform as the name of the king of Egypt who had recently died. Akhenaten's prenomen, Neferkheperure had been transliterated as "Naphurriya", as Egyptian "nfr" was surely vocalized as "Nafe" [final /r/ silent] at the time. Tutankhamun having no children, his wife, Ankhesenamun, descendant of pharaohs, had a legitimate claim to the throne and, insofar as we know, far better than that of the presumptuous Ay. The queen who wrote to the Hittites stated that her husband had no son. However, one never knew exactly how many sons an Egyptian pharaoh can have had by lesser wives and concubines, so the king of Hatti quite scrupulously was not willing to take the word of the queen. Therefore, he sent an envoy to Egypt to investigate the matter.

A faience ring[113] displays the name of Ay coupled with that of Ankhesenamun. It is merely her name, without either "king's wife" or "king's daughter" seen there. This has been construed as a sign of Ankhesenamun having married Ay, her own grandfather.

Can Ay have been the grandfather of that particular Ankhesenamun, if she was Tutankhamun's niece? Perhaps, but we do not know how that would have come about.

At one time I felt sure that Nefertiti could be identified via the mitochrondrial DNA of a foetus from KV62. I took it for granted that the queen, her daughter, Ankhesenamun, and the babies would all have the same mtDNA. As matters stand, that ought still to hold true, no matter if the chief wife of Tutankhamun was the elder Ankhesenpaaten or the younger. But I never expected the KV35YL to have been a daughter of Queen Tiye and a granddaughter of Thuya. Nor did I anticipate Tutankhamun could have had those children with another, unknown, female bearing different mtDNA—if, in fact, she did. It has become complex and, while there are some who probably know the truth of the matter, I am not one of them. So I will have to wait and see with the rest of you what will come out in the future.

I can only speculate that the same family from which Amunhotep III acquired a spouse might not have been neglected by Tutankhamun, either. Exactly why

---

113 The Newberry ring.

that would have been is also quite unclear, but there seems to be some connection to great-grandma Thuya, whoever she was. If that is the case, then the mtDNA of KV21A [or another girl] **could** still be the same as any daughter of the KV35YL, if she is Nefertiti.

God's Father Ay was hardly less important in the reign of Tut than during that of Akhenaten. In that event, the young pharaoh would not very surprisingly have taken a daughter or granddaughter of Ay into his harem. A relationship of Ay or Tey to Thuya would not be unexpected, either. On the other hand, Thuya can have had siblings who were great men, whose names we do not know. Or perhaps we know of them, but do not understand their connection to Thuya. The odds are good that the mother of Queen Tiye was not the only person in Egypt to bear the same alleles as she at some of the loci, those same numbers not inherited by Tiye. At the time of King Thutmose IV, officials like Sobekhotep and Menna, for example, had daughters who were concubines of that pharaoh.[114] Tut may have followed suit, taking the daughters of important men into his harem once he was old enough to do so.

Were there ever mummies of commoner individuals who were relatives of Nefertiti and her extended family? I would say that it was quite likely. At the Theban necropolis, much of the hill Sheikh abd el-Qurna was taken up by the tombs of generations of

---

114 The only other child ascribed to Thuya other than Tiye was that man called Aanen, who was Second Prophet of Amun, sm-priest of Heliopolis, and [yet another] God's Father. He seems to have died around Year 34 of Amunhotep III but had a son and some daughters.

members of one very important family, which supplied the 18th Dynasty with viziers and priests. When the savants of Napoleon Bonaparte came to Egypt, they explored the ancient cemetery, bringing back with them two mummified heads, one male and one female, said to be from "the environs of Quorneh". They were painted by a fine artist in the age before photography and included in the tome, "Description de l'Egypte". The heads were, at least at one time, in an excellent state of preservation. The one of the woman struck me, long ago, as having quite a resemblance, in the profile view, to the little wooden head of Queen Tiye.

It was given as a present to Josephine, wife of Napoleon Bonaparte, by explorer, Vivant Denon. After Josephine's death, the item was reclaimed by Denon for the Paris Louvre. Perhaps the heads are still somewhere in the museum.

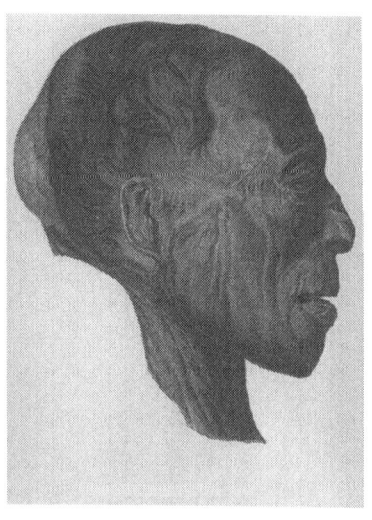

When the queen of Egypt wrote to King Suppiluliuma that she did not want to marry one of her servants, she may have included Ay, as there really is no proof that he was any blood relation to the young widow. It is all speculation at this point. Moreover, rings were not necessarily associated with marriage in ancient Egypt. The two names, side by side, may have merely been a case of yet more propaganda. At the instigation of Ay, the cheap trinkets were made as souvenirs, demonstrating that the widow of King Tutankhamun endorsed Ay as his successor.

Obviously, Ankhesenamun endorsed no one and her correspondence with the Hittite ruler was probably a surreptitious one if she resided at Memphis [or elsewhere] and Ay in the south. The queen may even have had the opportunity to receive an envoy of

Suppiluliuma without King Ay being any the wiser. At any rate, this royal lady certainly seems to have indicated that the right to kingship was derived from and through her as she wrote: *"He who was my husband is dead and I have no son. Should I then perhaps take one of my servants and make of him my husband? I have written to no other country; I have written to you. They say that you have many sons. Give me one of your sons and he will be my husband and lord of the land of Egypt."*

Mursili II, a successor of Suppiluliuma, is the source of the information about the "Zannanza affair", that being the name of the ill-fated prince sent to Egypt at the request of the widowed queen. He claimed that the woman wrote to Hatti for a husband as the Egyptians were afraid of the Hittites and wished for an alliance with them instead of possible conquest. But it is all filtered through the memory and perspective of Mursili, who was quite young when the events occurred. Regardless, it would seem that Ay was involved because the correspondence between a king of Egypt and an enraged Suppiluliuma points to the Hittite ruler having no idea that there was a man who had any right to the Egyptian throne at that time.

" .... I was ready to send my son to be king. But you were already on the throne and I did not know. Concerning what you have written to me: 'Your son has died, but I have not caused him any ill.' When the queen of Egypt wrote me again, you did not ... But if you had ascended to the throne in the meanwhile, you should have sent my son back to his home ... your servant Hani[115] *holds*

---

115 Hani had been a royal diplomat since the days of Akhenaten. Is it

186

us responsible...What have you done with my son?"

King Mursili, whose land was in the throes of a terrible pestilence, laid some of the blame at the feet of Suppiluliuma. He apparently felt his father should never have encroached on Egyptian territory in the first place because there was a treaty in place. Dishonor brought bad luck in the estimation of Mursili. However, in the end, Mursili seems to have found out what transpired with his brother, Zannanza. He had never even made it to Egypt.

"...My father sent foot soldiers and charioteers who attacked the country of Amqa, Egyptian territory. Again he sent troops and they attacked it. When the Egyptians became frightened, they asked outright for one of his sons to [take over] the kingship. But when my father gave them one of his sons, they killed him as they led him there. My father let his anger run away with him, he went to war against Egypt and attacked Egypt. The Hattian Storm-god, my lord, by his decision even let my father prevail; he vanquished and smote foot soldiers and the charioteers of the country of Egypt. But when they brought to Hatti land the prisoners which they had taken a plague broke out among the prisoners and they began to die."

On this somber note ends the saga of Nefertiti, Akhenaten, and their children inasmuch as can be presently known. Once again, matters seem to be at an impasse. I have written to Egypt, making it clear that our knowledge of the 18th Dynasty cannot go forward without

possible he had turned traitor to Queen Ankhesenamun and revealed her negotiations to Ay?

187

being able to view the autosomal DNA of King Thutmose IV. It is up to the Egyptians to decide how much the world can know of the most arcane, those secret things that cannot be uncovered by digging into the ground or discovering a hidden chamber somewhere. The mysteries of Egypt are now in the hands of people in white coats and masks and the laboratory is their domain.

I will continue thinking about Nefertiti, her family and her circumstances. I know that being right or wrong does not matter. Only the facts are important. I only hope for more proof to serve the truth.

47915869R00110

Made in the USA
Lexington, KY
17 December 2015